Anonymous

Hymns and Songs for Catholic children

Anonymous

Hymns and Songs for Catholic children

ISBN/EAN: 9783337265465

Printed in Europe, USA, Canada, Australia, Japan

Cover: Foto ©Lupo / pixelio.de

More available books at **www.hansebooks.com**

Hymns and Songs

Catholic Children.

NEW YORK:
THE CATHOLIC PUBLICATION SOCIETY,
9 BARCLAY STREET.

Entered according to Act of Congress in the year 1870, by

CATHOLIC PUBLICATION SOCIETY CO.,

In the Clerk's Office of the District Court of the United States for the Southern District of New York.

PREFACE.

This volume has been compiled to meet a want long felt in this parish, and at the expressed desire of many other pastors.

It furnishes a choice selection of hymns, in good type, and at a price within the reach of every child. The writer designs to publish soon a cheap and popular book of music, arranged for these hymns.

The author submits it to those entrusted with the instruction of the young, hoping it may assist them in their arduous work.

CHURCH OF ST. PAUL THE APOSTLE,
    Fifty-ninth St., New York,
        EASTER, 1870.

CONTENTS.

	PAGE
A solemn Hymn of Thanksgiving (*44)..........	9
All hail ! the power of Jesus' Name (*85).......	97
All ye who groan beneath (*148)...............	150
Angels we have heard on High (*76)............	21
At the Cross her Station keeping...............	61
As pants the Hart for cooling Streams..........	88
Ave Maris Stella (Latin)......................	46
Ave Maris Stella (English)....................	137
Blessed be the Love of Jesus...................	81
Blest is the Faith, divine and strong...........	178
Brightly gleams our Banner...	201
Blest Spirits of Light (*123)...................	158
By th' Archangel's Word of Love...............	15
Commandments of the Church (*170)..........	171
Christians, to the War !......................	186
Come, Holy Ghost, who ever one (*111).........	73
Come, Holy Ghost, Creator blest...............	72
Christmas Carol (*79).........................	23
Day of Wrath ! O Day of Mourning !.	12
Daily, daily sing to Mary.....................	136
Dear Husband of Mary (*178).................	148
Evening (*190)...	194
From the highest Heights of Glory.............	152
Faith of our Fathers..........................	179

Contents.

	PAGE
First Floweret of the Desert Wild	157
Full in the panting Heart of Rome	177
Great God, we thank Thee	175
Gentle Star of Ocean (*139)	137
Glory be to Jesus (*116)	95
God rest ye, merry Gentlemen (*79)	24
God of Mercy and Compassion	43
God bless our Pope	177
Hymn in Honor of the Blessed Sacrament (*51)	74
Holy God, we praise Thy Name (*44)	9
Hark, hark, my Soul, angelic Songs are swelling	164
Hear Thy Children, gentle Jesus	196
Happy we who, thus united	175
Hail, Queen of Heaven!	138
Hail, Thou living Bread from Heaven! (*48)	84
Hail, Virgin of Virgins! (*119)	120
Hail, Virgin! dearest Mary (*136)	141
Hail, Ocean Star! (*90)	113
Hail, bright Star of Ocean!	126
Hail, Holy Mission!	200
Holy Patron, thee Saluting (*146)	146
Heart of the Holy Child	102
Heaven is the Prize	169
Hail, holy Joseph	149
Hark! the Herald Angels sing	69
Hymn of the Passion	55

Contents.

	PAGE
Infant's Hymn to the Blessed Virgin Mary (*122).	112
I saw three Ships come sailing in	33
In Bethlehem Town He lay Him down (*82)	36
I am a little Catholic (*165)	181
I met the Good Shepherd (*159)	162
Infant Jesus, meek and mild	102
I'll never forsake Thee, I never will be	180
Invocation to the Holy Ghost	72
Jesus subject to His Parents	101
Jesus, ever-loving Saviour	58
Jesus, my Lord, my God, my All (*46)	80
Jesus, gentlest Saviour (*62)	91
Jesus, the very Thought of Thee (*86)	98
Jesus Christ is risen to-day (*106)	71
Jesus, Jesus, come to me	89
Joy, Joy, the Mother comes	117
Lead me to Thy peaceful Manger	32
Let the deep Organ swell the Lay	156
Little Children, Hail the Morn (*122)	112
Litany of the Blessed Virgin	143
Lauda Sion Salvatorem (*51)	74
Magnificat! Inspired Word (*118)	115
Mother Mary, at thine Altar (*141)	130
Maiden Mother, meek and mild	129
Mary, Mother! shield us	132
My Jesus, say, what Wretch has dared?	47

Contents.

	PAGE
Mary to the Saviour's Tomb..................	68
May Jesus Christ be praised...................	99
Nearer, my God, to Thee (*161)...............	166
Now with the fast departing Light (*191).......	195
Our Father who art in Heaven.................	207
O divinest Childhood ! (*75)..................	30
O Paradise ! O Paradise ! (*173)..............	168
O Jesus Christ! remember (*50)...............	90
Oh ! sing a joyous Carol (*78)................	28
O Jerusalem beloved ! (*88)...................	37
One God alone thou shalt adore (*170).........	171
Oh ! come and mourn with me (*93)...........	56
Oft in Danger, oft in Woe (*152)..............	188
O Jesus, God and Man ! (*158)................	103
Oh ! how much I love that sweet Story (*172)...	101
O Vault of Heaven, clear and bright...........	85
Oh ! balmy and bright........................	125
O lovely Voices of the Sky....................	27
O God of Mercy ! pity us.....................	42
Our Native Land..............................	206
On Sundays, Holydays likewise................	172
Once in Royal David's City (*206).............	20
O Sons and Daughters, let us sing (*104).......	63
Oh ! come to the merciful Saviour.............	198
O Christ ! Thy guilty People spare............	15
O'erwhelmed in Depths of Woe (*100)..........	55

Contents.

	PAGE
Oh! turn those blessed Points	60
Onward! Christian Soldiers	204
Once more the solemn Season calls	41
O Salutaris Hostia (*65)	209
O purest of Creatures	109
O Mary, my Mother! most lovely, most mild	135
O Child of God, remember (*155)	185
Oh! turn to Jesus, Mother, turn	107
Our Evening Hymn (*188)	197
O Maria, sine Labe concepta	112
Praises of the Blessed Sacrament	85
Rock of Ages, rent for me (*117)	96
St. Rose of Lima	157
School Hymn (*158)	103
St. Mary Magdalene	152
Saint Joseph (*146)	146
Saint Paul (*148)	150
See, He comes whom every Nation (*69)	11
See, amid the Winter's Snow (*71)	17
Saint Agnes, holy Child (*151)	154
Smile Praises, O Sky! (*108)	66
Snow and Rain have vanished (*137)	123
Star of Jacob, ever beaming (*121)	122
Star of the Ocean, hail! (*141)	128
Sweet Saviour, bless us ere we go (*188)	197
See! the Morning Star is dwelling (*204)	19

	PAGE
Sing the Battle sharp and glorious (*202)	67
Sing, sing, ye Angel Bands	118
Sweet Angel of Mercy (*124)	159
Summer's Departure (*198)	189
Stabat Mater	61
Tantum Ergo	209
The most Holy Sacrifice	87
The Seven Dolors	62
The Spear and the Nails	60
The Stations of the Cross	49
Three Knights of Orient	39
Thou loving Maker of Mankind	54
The Magnificat	115
The precious Blood	95
The Resurrection	63
The Snow lay on the Ground (*79)	23
The Leaves around me falling (*197)	190
The glory of Summer has faded and fled (*198)	189
Then thou hast conquered, then at last (*192)	192
Two thousand Years ago (*166)	182
The Son of God came down from Heaven (*94)	49
There sat a Lady all on the Ground (*140)	140
The joyous Birds are singing	124
The Night is come (*190)	194
This is the Image of the Queen (*134)	133
The Cross! the Cross!	44

Contents.

	PAGE
The Church has Seven Sacraments	173
The Name of Jesus	97
The Lord's Prayer	207
The Sinner invited to the Mission	198
The Commendation (*191)	195
The Sign of the Cross (*155)	185
The Church of the Saints	180
The Seven Sacraments	173
The Presentation in the Temple, on Candlemas Day	37
The Souls of the Faithful	104
The Pilgrim Queen of Merry England (*140)	140
The Patronage of St. Joseph	148
To St. Cæcilia	156
The Good Shepherd	162
The Pilgrims of the Night	164
The Commandments	171
Te Deum Laudamus	9
What Happiness can equal mine? (*58)	93
What lovely Infant can this be? (*73)	26
When the loving Shepherd	78
When the Patriarch was returning	87
We three Kings of Orient are	39
When Morning gilds the Skies	99
What a Sea of Tears and Sorrows!	62
When I Survey the wondrous Cross	53

Contents.

	PAGE
Ye Souls of the Faithful	104
Yes, Heaven is the Prize	169

Adoro Te	211
Ave Verum	211
Close veiled in that sweet Sacrament	226
Holy Spirit ! Lord of Light !	223
Hymn for Apostles	230
Hymn for a Bishop or a Confessor	231
Hymn for Holy Women	233
Hymn for a Martyr	230
Hymn on the Passion	236
Hymn for Virgins	232
Jerusalem, my happy Home	235
Jerusalem, thou City Blest	234
Jesus, I my Cross have Taken	227
Majesty Divine	221
O come, O come, Emmanuel	222
O cor Jesu	211
O Vision bright ! (*229)	229
O Wounded Heart !	225
The Sodality Office	212

NOTE.—All the Hymns marked with an asterisk (*) and figure will be found set to appropriate Music in Father Young's *Catholic Hymns and Canticles* ; the figure denotes the page of that work.

HYMNS AND SONGS

FOR

Catholic Children.

TE DEUM LAUDAMUS.

A SOLEMN HYMN OF THANKSGIVING.

HOLY God, we praise Thy Name!
   Lord of all, we bow before Thee!
All on earth Thy sceptre claim,
   All in Heaven above adore Thee;
     Infinite Thy vast domain,
     Everlasting is Thy reign.

Hark! the loud celestial hymn
   Angel choirs above are raising!
Cherubim and Seraphim,
   In unceasing chorus praising,

Fill the heavens with sweet accord:
Holy ! Holy ! Holy Lord !

Lo ! the Apostolic train
  Join, thy sacred name to hallow !
Prophets swell the loud refrain,
  And the white-robed Martyrs follow:
    And from morn to set of sun,
    Through the Church the song goes on.

Holy Father, Holy Son,
  Holy Spirit, Three we name Thee,
While in essence only One
  Undivided God, we claim Thee ;
    And adoring bend the knee,
    While we own the mystery.

Thou art King of Glory, Christ !
  Son of God, yet born of Mary ;
For us sinners sacrificed,
  And to death a tributary ;
    First to break the bars of death,
    Thou hast open'd Heaven to Faith.

From Thy high celestial home,
  Judge of all, again returning,

We believe that Thou shalt come,
  On the dreadful Doomsday morning,
    When Thy voice shall shake the earth,
    And the startled dead come forth.

Spare Thy people, Lord! we pray,
  By a thousand snares surrounded;
Keep us without sin to-day,
  Never let us be confounded.
    Lo! I put my trust in Thee,
    Never, Lord, abandon me.

Walworth T.

ADVENT.

SEE HE COMES.

SEE, He comes! whom every nation,
  Taught of God, desired to see;
Fill'd with hope and expectation
  That He would their Saviour be.
Sing, oh! sing with exultation,
  Haste we to our Father's home;
Peace, redemption, joy, salvation,
  Now from Heaven to earth are come.

See, He comes! whom kings and sages,
    Prophets, patriarchs of old,
Distant climes, and countless ages,
    Waited eager to behold.
Sing, oh! sing with exultation,
    Haste we to our Father's home;
Peace, redemption, joy, salvation,
    Now from Heaven to earth are come.

See the Lamb of God appearing,
    God of God, from Heaven above!
See the Heavenly Bridegroom cheering
    His dear Bride with words of love!
Glory to th' Eternal Father,
    Glory to th' Incarnate Son,
Glory to the Holy Spirit,
    Glory to the Three in One!

DAY OF WRATH! O DAY OF MOURNING!

DAY of wrath! O day of mourning!
    See fulfilled the prophets' warning!
Heaven and earth doth pass away!

Oh! what fear man's bosom rendeth,
When from Heaven the Judge descendeth,
Just and sinners to repay.

Hark, the trumpet-blast appalling!
On the grave's deep stillness falling,
Small and great the summons hear.

And the buried generations,
People of all times and nations,
Stand before the Throne in fear.

Lo, the Book exactly worded!
Wherein all hath been recorded,
Shall be held before our sight.

When that Court shall hold its session,
Every mouth shall make confession,
Every deed be brought to light.

What shall I, frail man, be pleading,
Who for me be interceding,
When the just of help have need?

Awful King of earth and heaven,
Thou to me Thy grace hast given,
Let Thy mercy for me plead.

Blessed Jesus, our salvation
Caused Thy wondrous Incarnation,
Thee Thy Cross and Passion cost.

Guilty now, we pour our moaning,
All our shame with anguish owning,
Jesus, let me not be lost!

Thou the sinful woman savedst,
Thou the dying thief forgavest,
Pardon also grant to me.

When thou makest separation,
With Thy sheep assign my station,
Safe from hell's dark misery.

Day of weeping and of wailing!
Human hearts and fates unveiling!
Day when sinners may despair!

Then, oh! then, from my long slumber,
Standing, trembling, 'mid that number,
Spare me, God of mercy, spare!

O CHRIST, THY GUILTY PEOPLE SPARE.

O CHRIST, Thy guilty people spare;
  Lo, kneeling at Thy gracious throne,
Thy Virgin Mother pours her prayer,
  Imploring pardon for her own.

Ye Prophets and Apostles high,
  Behold our contrite sighs and tears;
And plead for us when death is nigh,
  And our all-searching Judge appears.

Ye Martyrs all, a purple band,
  And Confessors, a white-robed train;
Oh! call us to our native land
  From this, our exile, back again.

Drive from the flocks, O spirits blest!
  The false and faithless race away;
That all within one fold may rest,
  Secure beneath one shepherd's sway!

BY TH' ARCHANGEL'S WORD OF LOVE.

BY th' Archangel's word of love,
  That announced Thee from above,
By the grace to Mary given,

By Thy first descent from Heaven,
Now, when Thou to us dost say,
"Meet me on the Judgment Day"—
Child of Mary, hear our prayer,
Help us sinners to prepare.

By that journey made in haste,
O'er the desert mountain waste,
By that voice whose heavenly word,
Yet unborn the Baptist heard,
Now, when Thou to us dost say,
"Meet me on the Judgment Day"—
Child of Mary, hear our prayer,
Help us sinners to prepare.

By thy poor and lowly lot,
By the manger and the grot,
By thy infant feet and hands,
Folded in the swathing bands,
Now, when Thou to us dost say,
"Meet me on the Judgment Day"—
Child of Mary, hear our prayer,
Help us sinners to prepare.

By the joy of Simeon blest,
When he clasped Thee to his breast,

By the widow'd Anna's song,
Pour'd amid the wondering throng,
Now, when Thou to us dost say,
"Meet me on the Judgment Day"—
Child of Mary, hear our prayer,
Help us sinners to prepare.

CHRISTMAS.

SEE, AMID THE WINTER'S SNOW.

SEE, amid the winter's snow,
  Born for us on earth below ;
Christ our Lord is born for us on earth below.
See, the tender Lamb appears,
Promised from eternal years !
    Sing thro' all Jerusalem,
    Christ is born in Bethlehem ;
    Sing Christ our Lord is born a child in
      Bethlehem.
  Chorus.—Hail, thou ever-blessed morn !
    Hail, Redemption's happy dawn !
      Sing thro' all, etc.

Lo ! within a manger lies
He who built the starry skies ;
Mary's child is he who built the starry skies.
He who, thron'd in height sublime,
Sits amid the Cherubim !
Chorus.—Hail, etc.

Say, ye holy shepherds, say,
What your joyful news to-day ?
What can be your glad and joyful news to-day ?
Wherefore have ye left your sheep
On the lonely mountain steep ?
Chorus.—Hail, etc.

" As we watched at dead of night,
Lo ! we saw a wondrous light ;
High in heaven, lo ! we saw a wondrous light ;
Angels singing, ' Peace on earth !'
Told us of the Saviour's birth."
Chorus.—Hail, etc.

Sacred Infant, all divine,
What a tender love was Thine !

Blessed Saviour, what a tender love was Thine!
Thus to come from highest bliss
Down to such a world as this!
      Chorus.—Hail, etc.

Teach, oh! teach us, Holy Child,
By Thy face so meek and mild,
By Thy sacred little face so meek and mild—
Teach us to resemble Thee
In Thy sweet humility.
      Chorus.—Hail, etc.

Virgin Mother, Mary blest,
By the joys that fill thy breast,
By the flood of heavenly joys that fill thy breast,
Pray for us, that we may prove
Worthy of our Saviour's love.
      Chorus.—Hail, etc.

SEE! THE MORNING STAR IS DWELLING.

SEE! the morning star is dwelling
 On the eastern mountain's height;
See! the day all days excelling
 Bursts upon our aching sight.

Sing we then our carol free,
Christus Natus, Natus Hodie.

Long our watch has been, and dreary,
Long we wandered from afar,
So the wise men, worn and weary,
Followed still the leading star,
Till the Day-spring's self they see,
Christus Natus, Natus Hodie.

Hence, away! all care and sadness!
Hence, and ne'er return again!
Angels sing with notes of gladness,
"Peace on earth, good-will to men;'
Join we then in carol free,
Christus Natus, Natus Hodie.

ONCE IN ROYAL DAVID'S CITY.

ONCE in royal David's city
  Stood a lowly cattle-shed,
Where a mother laid her Baby,
  In a manger for His bed.
    Mary was that mother mild,
    Jesus Christ her little child.

He came down to earth from Heaven
　Who is God and Lord of all,
And His shelter was a stable,
　And His cradle was a stall;
　　With the poor, and mean, and lowly,
　　Lived on earth our Saviour holy.

And our eyes at last shall see Him,
　Through his own redeeming love,
For that Child so dear and gentle,
　Is our Lord in Heaven above.
　　And He leads His children on,
　　To the place where He is gone.

Not in that poor lowly stable,
　With the oxen slumbering by,
We shall see Him; but in Heaven,
　Set at God's right hand on high;
　　When, like stars, His children crowned
　　All in white, shall wait around.

C. F. Alexander

ANGELS WE HAVE HEARD ON HIGH.

ANGELS we have heard on high,
   Sweetly singing o'er our plains,
And the mountains in reply,
   Echo back their joyous strains;
     Sing, oh! sing, this blessed morn,
     Jesus Christ to-day is born.
Chorus.—Gloria in excelsis Deo! *(Twice.)*

Shepherds, why this jubilee?
   Why your rapturous strain prolong?
Say, what may the tidings be,
   Which inspire your heavenly song?
     Sing, oh! sing, etc.

Come to Bethlehem, come and see
   Him whose birth the angels sing;
Come, adore on bended knee,
   Th' Infant Christ, the new-born King.
     Sing, oh! sing, etc.

See, within a manger laid,
   Jesus, Lord of Heaven and earth!
Mary, Joseph, lend your aid,
   With us sing our Saviour's birth.
     Sing, oh! sing, etc.

CHRISTMAS CAROL.

THE snow lay on the ground,
  The star shone bright,
When Christ our Lord was born
  On Christmas night.
    Venite adoremus Dominum. *(Twice.)*

'Twas Mary, daughter pure
  Of holy Anne,
That brought into this world
  The God-made man.
    Venite adoremus Dominum. *(Twice.)*

She laid him in a stall,
  At Bethlehem,
The ass and oxen shared
  The roof with them.
    Venite adoremus Dominum. *(Twice.)*

Saint Joseph, too, was by,
  To tend the Child,
To guard Him and protect
  His mother mild.
    Venite adoremus Dominum. *(Twice.)*

The angels hovered round,
  And sung this song,
Venite adoremus
  Dominum.
    Venite adoremus Dominum. (Twice.)

And then that manger poor
  Became a throne:
For He, whom Mary bore,
  Was God the Son.
    Venite adoremus Dominum. (Twice.)

O come, then, let us join
  The Heavenly host,
To praise the Father, Son,
  And Holy Ghost.
    Venite adoremus Dominum. (Twice.)

GOD REST YE, MERRY GENTLEMEN.

GOD rest ye, merry gentlemen, let nothing you dismay,
For Jesus Christ, our Saviour, was born on Christmas-day.

The dawn rose red o'er Bethlehem, the stars
    shone through the gray,
When Jesus Christ, our Saviour, was born on
    Christmas-day.

God rest ye, little children, let nothing you af-
    fright,
For Jesus Christ, our Saviour, was born this
    happy night;
Along the hills of Galilee the white flock sleep-
    ing lay,
When Christ, the Child of Nazareth, was born
    on Christmas-day.

God rest ye, all good Christians, upon this
    blessed morn,
The Lord of all good Christians was of a wo-
    man born;
Now all your sorrows He doth heal, your sins
    He takes away;
For Jesus Christ, our Saviour, was born on
    Christmas-day.

WHAT LOVELY INFANT CAN THIS BE!

WHAT lovely Infant can this be, } *Twice.*
    That in the little crib I see? }
So sweetly on the straw it lies— } *Twice.*
It must have come from Paradise. }

Who is that Lady kneeling by, } *Twice.*
And gazing on, so tenderly? }
Oh! that is Mary, ever blest, } *Twice.*
How full of joy her holy breast! }

What man is that who seems to smile } *Twice.*
And look so blissful all the while? }
'Tis holy Joseph, good and true; } *Twice.*
The Infant makes him happy too. }

What makes the crib so bright and
    clear? } *Twice.*
What voices sing so sweetly here? }
Ah! see, behind the window-pane, } *Twice.*
The little angels looking in! }

Who are those people kneeling down,
With crooked sticks and hands so } *Twice.*
    brown?

The shepherds on the mountain-top,
The little angels woke them up.

The ox and ass, how still and mild
They stand beside the Holy Child;
They warm so kindly with their breath
His little body underneath.

Hail, holy cave! though dark thou be,
The world is lighted up from thee.
Hail, Holy Babe! creation stands,
And moves upon Thy little hands.

O LOVELY VOICES OF THE SKY!

   LOVELY voices of the sky!
    That hymned the Saviour's birth,
Are ye not singing still on high
    Who once sang "Peace on earth"?
Still o'er us float those holy strains
    Wherewith, in days gone by,
Ye blessed the lowly Syrian swains—
    O voices of the sky!

O clear and shining light! whose beams
　A heavenly radiance shed
Around the palms and o'er the streams,
　And on the shepherd's head,
Be near through life, be near in death,
　As in that holiest night
Of hope, of gladness, and of faith—
　O clear and shining light!

O star which ledst to Him whose love
　Brought down man's ransom free!
Thou still art 'midst the hosts above;
　We still may gaze on thee.
In heaven thy light doth never set;
　Thy rays earth may not dim.
Oh! send them forth to guide us yet,
　Bright star which led to Him.

Mrs Hemans

OH! SING A JOYOUS CAROL.

OH! sing a joyous carol
　Unto the Holy Child,
And praise with gladsome voices
　His Mother undefiled.

Our youthful voices, greeting,
　　Shall hail our infant King,
And our sweet Lady listens
　　When children's voices sing.

Who is there meekly lying
　　In yonder stable poor?
Dear children, it is Jesus;
　　He bids you now adore.
Who is there kneeling by Him
　　In virgin beauty fair?
It is our Mother Mary;
　　She bids you all draw near.

Who is there near the manger
　　That guards the holy Child?
It is the great St. Joseph,
　　Chaste spouse of Mary mild.
Dear children, oh! how joyful
　　With them in heaven to be!
God grant that none be missing
　　From that festivity.

O DIVINEST CHILDHOOD!

 DIVINEST childhood
   Of my Saviour dear!
How, in very weakness,
   Does His strength appear!
How Thy beauty, Jesu,
   Ravishes my heart!
How, the more abased,
   The greater still Thou art.

Hither speed, ye angels,
   On exultant wing;
View, in this poor manger,
   Heaven's eternal King.
Ah! by faith instructed,
   How I joy to see
These first tears of pity
   Which He sheds for me.

O mysterious silence!
   Eloquence Divine!
O exact obedience!
   Would that such were mine!

Near our little Jesus
　　Docile grows my mind,
Nor can aught perplexing
　　In His Gospel find.

Does not this sweet Infant
　　Seem to thee to say,
Cast thy heartless trusting
　　In thyself away.
Know that if thou learn not
　　To resemble Me,
Happiness celestial
　　Ne'er can fall on thee.

" Come, ye little children,
　　Unto Me draw nigh ;
For 'tis such as you that
　　Dwell with Me on high,
Who, in love and meekness,
　　From all malice free,
Serve their dear Redeemer
　　With simplicity.

" I, who pride and greatness
　　Evermore abase,
On the poor and lowly
　　Lavish all my grace,

And to humble spirits
　　Heavenly things reveal,
Which My secret judgments
　　From the proud conceal"?

Thus, O sweetest Jesu!
　　Seemest Thou to say,
"Ah! then, wretched worldlings,
　　Cast your pride away.
If the God of glory
　　So himself abase,
How shall man presume to
　　Choose the highest place?

LEAD ME TO THY PEACEFUL MANGER.

LEAD me to Thy peaceful manger,
　　Wondrous Babe of Bethlehem.
Shepherds hail Thee, yet a stranger;
　　Let me worship Thee with them.
I am vile, but Thou art holy.
　　Oh! unite my heart to Thee,
Make me contrite, keep me lowly,
　　Pure as Thou wouldst have me be.

Let me listen to the story,
　Full of all-surpassing love,
How the Lord of grace and glory
　Left for us His throne above.
Touched with sympathy so tender,
　Man adores while seraphs gaze,
And with gladness we surrender
　Soul and body to Thy praise.

Blessed Jesus, holy Saviour,
　Offspring of the royal Maid,
By Thy meek and pure behavior
　In her folding arms displayed,
By the tears of earliest anguish
　On Thine infant brow impearled,
By the love that could not languish,
　Thou hast saved a ruined world.

I SAW THREE SHIPS.

I SAW three ships come sailing in,
　On Christmas day,
　On Christmas day;
I saw three ships come sailing in,
　On Christmas day in the morning.

And what were in those ships all three?
   On Christmas day,
   On Christmas day;
And what were in those ships all three
   On Christmas day in the morning?

Our Saviour Christ and His Ladye,
   On Christmas day,
   On Christmas day;
Our Saviour Christ and His Ladye,
   On Christmas day in the morning.

Pray whither sailed those ships all three?
   On Christmas day,
   On Christmas day;
Pray whither sailed those ships all three
   On Christmas day in the morning?

Oh! they sailed into Bethlehem,
   On Christmas day,
   On Christmas day;
Oh! they sailed into Bethlehem,
   On Christmas day in the morning.

And all the bells on earth shall ring,
   On Christmas day,
   On Christmas day;

And all the bells on earth shall ring,
    On Christmas day in the morning.

And all the angels in heaven shall sing,
    On Christmas day,
    On Christmas day;
And all the angels in heaven shall sing,
    On Christmas day in the morning.

And all the souls on earth shall sing,
    On Christmas day,
    On Christmas day;
And all the souls on earth shall sing,
    On Christmas day in the morning.

Then let us all be full of joy,
    On Christmas day,
    On Christmas day;
Then let us all be full of joy,
    On Christmas day in the morning.

A merry, merry Christmas to you all,
    On Christmas day,
    On Christmas day;
A merry, merry Christmas to you all,
    On Christmas day in the morning.

EPIPHANY.

IN BETHLEHEM TOWN.

IN Bethlehem town He lay Him down,
  Within a place obscure.
O little Bethlehem! poor in walls,
  But rich in furniture.
Chorus.
      Since heaven is now come down below,
        Hither the angels fly.
      Hark how the heavenly voices sing
        Glory to God on high!

The news is spread, the shepherds heard,
  And troubled Salem's peace.
King Herod groaned upon his throne
  For fear his reign should cease.
      Chorus.—Since heaven, etc.

Wise kings from far beheld the star
  Which was their faithful guide
Until it pointed out the Babe,
  And Him they glorified.
      Chorus.—Since heaven, etc.

The blazing star did shine so far
  That all the world might see,
And nations bound in darkness found
  True light and liberty.
      Chorus.—Since heaven, etc.

O heaven and earth ! for Jesu's birth
  With sweetest tunes abound;
And everything for the great King
  With cheerful songs resound.
      Chorus.—And glory still be paid to Him,
        And to His Father praise,
      And honor to the Holy Ghost,
        In every place always.

THE PRESENTATION OF JESUS IN THE TEMPLE:
OR CANDLEMAS-DAY.

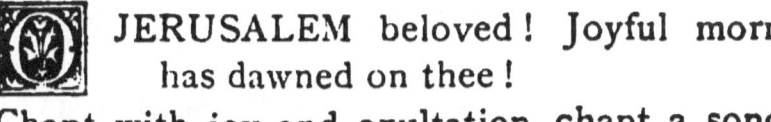JERUSALEM beloved ! Joyful morn
  has dawned on thee !
Chant with joy and exultation, chant a song
  of jubilee ;

For the Lord whom thou art seeking, He for whom the nations pray,
He, in human flesh appearing, to His temple comes to-day.

Glorious and bright the temple with its gold and silver shone
Which by royal hands was builded of the peaceful Solomon;
But thy latter house is brighter; for in it a heavenly Guest,
Son of David, everlasting Prince of Peace, is manifest.

He, the first-begotten only Son of God to-day is come;
He, the first-begotten only Son of holy Mary's womb.
All the faithful sons of Israel are in Him to God allied,
And, presented in the temple of the Lord, are sanctified.

Light the Gentile world to lighten, and the glory Israel,
Beams in Him, the heavenly Dayspring, God with us Emmanuel.

Now the aged world receives Him in its arms
    with faith's embrace,
And with Simeon rejoices in the sunshine of
    His grace.

May we, Lord, with holy Simeon, and with
    Anna, wait for Thee
In the visions of Thy temple! May our hearts
    Thy temple be!
So, with saints and holy angels, may we all for
    evermore
In Jerusalem, the heavenly, Thee, the Lord of
    all, adore!

C Wordsworth

THREE KINGS OF ORIENT.

WE three kings of Orient are.
    Bearing gifts we traverse afar
  Field and fountain,
  Moor and mountain,
Following yonder star.
Chorus.
  O Star of wonder, Star of night,
  Star with royal beauty bright!

Westward leading,
Still proceeding,
Guide us to Thy perfect light.

GASPARD:
Born a King on Bethlehem plain,
Gold I bring to crown Him again,
King for ever,
Ceasing never
Over us all to reign.
Chorus.—O Star of wonder! etc.

MELCHIOR:
Frankincense to offer have I;
Incense owns a Deity nigh.
Prayer and praising,
All men raising,
Worship Him, God on high.
Chorus.—O Star of Wonder! etc.

BALTHAZZAR
Myrrh is mine; its bitter perfume
Breathes a life of gathering gloom:
Sorrowing, sighing,
Bleeding, dying,
Sealed in the stone-cold tomb.
Chorus.—O Star of Wonder! etc.

Glorious now behold Him arise,
King, and God, and Sacrifice.
Heaven sings Alleluia,
Alleluia the earth replies.
Chorus.—O Star of Wonder! etc.

LENT.

ONCE MORE THE SOLEMN SEASON CALLS.

ONCE more the solemn season calls
   A holy fast to keep,
And now within the temple walls
   Both priest and people meet.

But vain all outward sign of grief,
   And vain the form of prayer,
Unless the heart implore relief
   And penitence be there.

We smite the breast, we weep in vain,
   In vain in ashes mourn,
Unless with penitential pain
   The smitten soul be torn.

In sorrow true, then, let us pray
    To our offended God
From us to turn His wrath away,
    And stay the uplifted rod.

O God! our Judge and Father, deign
    To spare the bruisèd reed;
We pray for time to turn again,
    For grace to turn indeed.

Blest Three in One, to thee we bow;
    Vouchsafe us in Thy love
To gather from these fasts below
    Immortal fruit above. Amen.

O GOD OF MERCY! PITY US.

O GOD of mercy! pity us,
    With weeping hearts we cry;
Do Thou then kindly pardon us,
    And hear Thy children's sigh.

My God, because Thou art so good,
    With sorrow I deplore
How I offended Thee by sin.
    I will offend no more. Amen.

for Catholic Children.

GOD OF MERCY AND COMPASSION.

GOD of mercy and compassion,
  Look with pity upon me.
Father—let me call Thee Father—
  'Tis Thy child returns to Thee.
Chorus.—Jesus, Lord, I ask for mercy ;
  Let me not implore in vain.
  All my sins I now detest **them;**
  Never will I sin again.

By my sins I have deservèd
  Death and endless misery,
Hell, with all its pains and **torments,**
  And for all eternity.
    Chorus.—Jesus, Lord, etc.

By my sins I have abandoned
  Right and claim to heaven **above,**
Where the saints rejoice for ever
  In a boundless sea of love.
    Chorus.—Jesus, Lord, etc.

See our Saviour, bleeding, dying,
  On the cross of Calvary.

To that cross my sins have nailed Him;
Yet He bleeds and dies for me.
Chorus.—Jesus, Lord, etc.

THE CROSS! THE CROSS!

THE Cross! the Cross! Oh! bid it rise
  'Mid clouds about it curled,
In bold relief against the skies,
  Beheld by all the world;
A sign to myriads far and wide
  On every holy fane,
Meet emblem of the Crucified,
  For our transgressions slain.

The Cross! the Cross! With solemn vow
  And fervent prayer to bless,
Upon the new-born infant's brow
  The hallowed seal impress;
A token that in coming years,
  All else esteemed but loss,
He will press on through foes and fears,
  The soldier of the Cross.

The Cross! the Cross! Upon the heart,
   Oh! seal the signet well,
A safeguard sweet against each art
   And stratagem of hell;
A hope when other hopes shall cease,
   And worth all hopes beside;
The Christian's blessedness and peace,
   His joy and only pride.

The Cross! the Cross! Ye heralds blest,
   Who, in the saving Name,
Go forth to lands with sin oppressed
   The Cross of Christ proclaim.
And so, 'mid idols lifted high,
   In truth and love revealed,
It may be seen by every eye,
   And stricken souls be healed.

The Cross! Dear Church, the world is dark,
   And wrapped in shades of night,
Yet, lift but up within thy ark,
   This source of living light--
This emblem of our heavenly birth,
   And claim to things Divine--
So thou shalt go through all the earth
   And conquer in this sign. Amen.

Hymns and Songs

AVE MARIS STELLA.

AVE maris stella
   Dei Mater alma,
Atque semper Virgo,
Felix cœli porta.

Sumens illud Ave
Gabrielis ore,
Funda nos in pace,
Mutans Evæ nomen.

Solve vincla reis,
Profer lumen cæcis,
Mala nostra pelle,
Bona cuncta posce.

Monstra te esse matrem,
Sumat per te preces,
Qui pro nobis Natus,
Tulit esse tuus.

Virgo singularis,
Inter omnes mitis,
Nos culpis solutus,
Mites fac et castos.

Vitam præsta puram,
Iter para tutum,
Ut videntes Jesum,
Semper collætemur.

Sit laus Deo Patri,
Summo Christo decus,
Spiritui Sancto,
Tribus honor unus.
                        Amen.]

MY JESUS, SAY, WHAT WRETCH HAS DARED?

MY Jesus, say what wretch has dared
    Thy sacred hands to bind?
And who has dared to buffet so
    Thy face so meek and kind?
Chorus.—'Tis I have thus ungrateful been;
    Yet, Jesus, pity take.
  Oh! spare and pardon me, my Lord,
    For Thy sweet mercy's sake.'

My Jesus, who with spittle vile
  Profaned Thy sacred brow?
And whose unpitying scourge has made
  Thy precious blood to flow?
    Chorus.—'Tis I, etc.

My Jesus, whose the hands that wove
  That cruel thorny crown?
Who made that hard and heavy cross
  Which weighs Thy shoulders down?
    Chorus.—'Tis I, etc.

My Jesus, who has mocked Thy thirst
  With vinegar and gall?
Who held the nails that pierced Thy hands,
  And made the hammer fall?
    Chorus.—'Tis I, etc.

My Jesus, say, who dared to nail
  Those tender feet of Thine?
And whose the arm that raised the lance
  To pierce that heart divine?
    Chorus.—'Tis I, etc.

And, Mary, who has murdered thus
  Thy loved and only One?

for Catholic Children. 49

Canst thou forgive the blood-stained hand
That robbed thee of thy Son?
Chorus.—'Tis I have thus ungrateful been
To Jesus and to thee.
Forgive me for thy Jesus' sake,
And pray to Him for me.

THE STATIONS OF THE CROSS.

THE Son of God came down from heaven,
Upon the earth to dwell,
And man condemns to cruel death
The Heart that loved him well.
Chorus.—Thou goest forth, O blessed Lord!
To suffer death for me;
And I, too, wish for Thee to live,
I wish to die for Thee.

2 He taketh up His heavy cross,
And bears the crushing load,
And as He meekly journeys on
His blood bedews the road.
Chorus.—Thou goest forth, etc.

3 Rude soldiers press and goad Him on·
   And straiten Him around,
And now beneath His weighty cross
   He falls upon the ground.
      Chorus.—Thou goest forth, etc.

4 His Mother hastens forth to join
   The Son she loved so well;
Their glances meet, their hearts are filled
   With grief no tongue can tell.
      Chorus.—Thou goest forth, etc

5 They fear the Saviour may expire
   Beneath His heavy load,
And Simon is compelled to bear
   His cross along the road.
      Chorus.—Thou goest forth, etc.

6 A Jewish woman wipes His face:
   Her pity to reward,
Upon her veil remains impressed
   An image of the Lord.
      Chorus.—Thou goest forth, etc.

7 The Saviour falls a second time,
   Oppressed with bitter pain;

The soldiers force Him to arise
And journey on again.
 Chorus.—Thou goest forth, etc.

8 The daughters of Jerusalem
Bewail His cruel fate;
He bids them for their children weep
Before it is too late.
 Chorus.—Thou goest forth, etc.

9 He's urged to move with quicker step;
His blood in torrents flows;
Again, again He falls to earth
Beneath their cruel blows.
 Chorus.—Thou goest forth, etc.

10 The soldiers strip with violence
The garments from His flesh,
And every wound He had received
Is made to bleed afresh.
 Chorus.—Thou goest forth, etc.

11 They lay Him down upon the cross,
They nail His hands and feet;
The cross is raised, and He is left
His coming death to meet.
 Chorus.—Thou goest forth, etc.

12 Three hours of agony had passed
   Since He was crucified;
His work was done, His hour was come—
He bowed His head, and died.
      Chorus.—Thou goest forth, etc

13 Now His disciples come and take
   The body from the cross;
His Mother folds it in her arms,
   And mourns her bitter loss.
      Chorus.—Thou goest forth, etc.

14 His followers bear Him to the tomb,
   Prepared with pious care,
Then, silently departing, leave
   The sacred body there.
      Chorus.—Thou goest forth, etc.

WHEN I SURVEY THE WONDROUS CROSS.

WHEN I survey the wondrous Cross
   On which the Prince of Glory died,
My richest gain I count but loss,
   And pour contempt on all my pride.

Forbid it, Lord, that I should boast
   Save in the Cross of Christ, my God;
All the vain things that charm me most,
   I sacrifice them to His Blood!

See, from His head, His hands, His feet,
   Sorrow and love flow mingling down;
Did e'er such love and sorrow meet,
   Or thorns compose so rich a crown?

Were the whole realm of nature mine,
   That were an offering all too small;
Love so amazing, so divine,
   Demands my life, my soul, my all.

To Christ, who won for sinners grace
   By bitter grief and anguish sore,
Be praise from all the ransomed race
   For ever and for evermore. Amen.

Watt,

THOU LOVING MAKER OF MANKIND.

THOU loving Maker of mankind,
   Before Thy throne we pray, we weep;
Oh! strengthen us with grace divine!
   Duly this sacred time to keep.

Great Judge of hearts, Thou dost discern
   Our ills, and all our weakness know;
Again to Thee with tears we turn,
   Again to us Thy mercy show.

Much have we sinned; but we confess
   Our guilt, and all our faults deplore:
Oh! for the praise of Thy great Name,
   Our fainting souls to health restore.

And grant us, while by fasts we strive
   This mortal body to control,
To fast from all the food of sin,
   And so to purify the soul.

Hear us, O Trinity thrice blest!
   Sole Unity, to Thee we cry;
Vouchsafe us from these fasts below
   To reap immortal fruit on high.

for Catholic Children. 55

HYMN OF THE PASSION.

'ERWHELM'D in depths of woe,
   Upon the tree of scorn
Hangs the Redeemer of mankind,
   With racking anguish torn.

See! how the nails those hands
   And feet so tender rend;
See! down His face, and neck, and **breast,**
   His sacred Blood descend.

Hark! with what awful cry
   His Spirit takes its flight;
That cry, it pierc'd His Mother's **heart,**
   And whelm'd her soul in night.

Earth hears, and to its base
   Rocks wildly to and fro;
Tombs burst; seas, rivers, mountains quake:
   The veil is rent in two.

The sun withdraws his light;
   The midday heav'ns grow pale;
The moon, the stars, the universe
   Their Maker's death bewail.

Shall man alone be mute?
  Come, youth, and hoary hairs!
Come, rich and poor! come, all mankind!
  And bathe those feet in tears.

Come! fall before His Cross,
  Who shed for us His blood;
Who died the victim of pure love,
  To make us sons of God.

Jesu! all praise to Thee,
  Our joy and endless rest!
Be Thou our guide while pilgrims here
  Our crown amid the blest.

Caswall.

OH! COME AND MOURN WITH ME AWHILE.

OH! come and mourn with me awhile;
  See, Mary calls us to her side;
Oh! come and let us mourn with her:
  Jesus, our Love, is crucified.

Have we no tears to shed for Him
  While soldiers scoff and Jews deride:
Ah, look how patiently He hangs!
  Jesus, our Love, is crucified.

Seven times He spoke seven words of love,
  And all three hours His silence cried
For mercy on the souls of men:
  Jesus, our Love, is crucified.

Come, take thy stand beneath the Cross,
  And let the blood from out that side
Fall gently on thee drop by drop:
  Jesus, our Love, is sacrificed.

A broken heart, a fount of tears—
  Ask, and they will not be denied;
A broken heart Love's cradle is:
  Jesus, our Love, is crucified.

O love óf God! O sin of man!
  In this dread act your strength is tried;
And victory remains with love:
  For He, our Love, is crucified.

Faber.

JESUS, EVER LOVING SAVIOUR.

JESUS, ever-loving Saviour,
   Thou didst live and die for me.
Living, I will live to love Thee;
   Dying, I will die for Thee.
      Jesus! Jesus!
By Thy life and death of sorrow,
   Help me in mine agony.

When the last dread hour approaching
   Fills my guilty soul with fear,
All my sins rise up before me,
   All my virtues disappear.
      Jesus! Jesus!
Turn not Thou in anger from me;
   Mary, Joseph, then be near.

Kindest Jesus, Thou wert standing
   By Thy foster-father's bed
While Thy mother, softly praying,
   Held her dying Joseph's head.
      Jesus! Jesus!
By that death so calm and holy,
   Soothe me in that hour of dread.

Mary, thou canst not forsake me,
    Virgin Mother undefiled ;
Thou didst not abandon Jesus,
    Dying, tortured, and reviled.
        Jesus ! Jesus !
Send Thy Mother to console me;
    Mary, help thy guilty child.

Jesus, when in cruel anguish,
    Dying on the shameful tree,
All abandoned by Thy Father,
    Thou didst writhe in agony—
        Jesus ! Jesus !
By those three long hours of sorrow
    Thou didst purchase hope for me.

When the priest, with holy unction,
    Prays for mercy and for grace,
May the tears of deep compunction
    All my guilty stains efface !
        Jesus ! Jesus !
Let me find in Thee a refuge,
    In Thy heart a resting-place.

Then, by all that Thou didst suffer,
    Grant me mercy in that day.

Help me, Mary, my sweet Mother;
Holy Joseph, near me stay.
Jesus! Jesus!
Let me die my lips repeating
Jesus, mercy! Mary, pray!

THE SPEAR AND THE NAILS.

OH! turn those blessed points, all bathed
In Jesus' blood, on me.
Mine were the sins that wrought His death;
Mine be the penalty.

Pierce through my feet, my hands, my heart;
So may some drop distil
Of blood divine into my soul,
And all its evils heal.

So shall my feet be slow to sin,
Harmless my hands shall be;
So from my wounded heart shall each
Forbidden passion flee.

Thee, Jesus, pierced with nails and spear,
Let every knee adore;
With Thee, O Father! and with Thee,
O Spirit! evermore.

AT THE CROSS HER STATION KEEPING.

(Stabat Mater.)

AT the cross her station keeping,
   Stood the mournful Mother, weeping,
  Close to Jesus to the last;

Through her heart, His sorrow sharing,
All His bitter anguish bearing,
  Now at length the sword had passed.

Oh! how sad and sore distressed
Was that Mother highly blessed
  Of the sole-begotten One!

Oh! that silent, ceaseless mourning!
Oh! those dim eyes never turning
  From that wondrous, suffering Son!

For His people's sins, the All-Holy
There she saw, a Victim lowly,
  Bleed in torments—bleed and die;

Saw the Lord's Anointed taken;
Saw her Child in death forsaken;
  Heard His last expiring cry.

Hymns and Songs

Those five wounds of Jesu smitten,
Mother, in my heart be written
  Deeply as in thine they be.

Thou, my Saviour's cross who bearest,
Thou, Thy Son's rebuke who sharest,
  Let me share them both with thee.

Caswall.

WHAT A SEA OF TEARS AND SORROWS!

(The Seven Dolors.)

WHAT a sea of tears and sorrows,
  Did the soul of Mary toss
To and fro upon its billows,
  While she wept her bitter loss,
In her arms her Jesus holding,
  Torn but newly from the cross!

Oh! that mournful Virgin Mother!
  See her tears how fast they flow
Down upon His mangled body,
  Wounded side, and thorny brow;
While His hands and feet she kisses—
  Picture of immortal woe—

for Catholic Children.   63

Oft and oft His arms and bosom
  Fondly straining to her own ;
Oft her pallid lips imprinting
  On each wound of her dear Son ;
Till at last, in swoons of anguish,
  Sense and consciousness are gone.

Gentle Mother, we beseech thee,
  By thy tears and trouble sore,
By the death of thy dear Offspring,
  By the bloody wounds He bore,
Touch our hearts with that true sorrow
  Which afflicted thee of yore.

EASTER.

THE RESURRECTION.

SONS and daughters! let us sing!
  The King of Heaven, the glorious King,
To-day is risen triumphing. Alleluia!
  Alleluia! Alleluia! Alleluia!

On Sunday morn, at break of day,
The faithful women went their way
To seek the tomb where Jesus lay. Alleluia!
   Alleluia! Alleluia! Alleluia!

An angel clad in white they see,
Who sat and spake unto the three—
"Your Lord doth go to Galilee." Alleluia!
   Alleluia! Alleluia! Alleluia!

That night the Apostles met in fear.
Amidst them came the Lord most dear,
And said, "My peace be on all here." Alleluia!
   Alleluia! Alleluia! Alleluia!

When Didymus the tidings heard,
He doubted if it were the Lord
Until He came and spake the word. Alleluia!
   Alleluia! Alleluia! Alleluia!

"My piercèd side, O Thomas! see;
My hands, My feet, I show to thee;
Not faithless, but believing be." Alleluia!
   Alleluia! Alleluia! Alleluia!

No longer Thomas then denied;
He saw the feet, the hands, the side;
"Thou art my Lord and God," he cried.
    Alleluia!
  Alleluia! Alleluia! Alleluia!

How blest are they who do not see
And yet whose faith is firm in Thee!
For they shall live eternally.   Alleluia!
  Alleluia! Alleluia! Alleluia!

On this most holy day of days
To Thee our heart and voice we raise
In laud, and jubilee, and praise.   Alleluia!
  Alleluia! Alleluia! Alleluia!

Glory to Father and to Son,
Who has for us the victory won!
And Holy Ghost! Blest Three in One!
    Alleluia!
  Alleluia! Alleluia! Alleluia!

Neale Tr.

Hymns and Songs

SMILE PRAISES, O SKY!

SMILE praises, O sky!
  Soft breathe them, O air!
Below and on high,
  And everywhere!
The black troop of storms
  Has yielded to calm,
Tufted blossoms are peeping,
  And early palm.

Arouse thee, O Spring!
  Ye flowers, come forth;
With thousand hues tinting
  The soft green earth;
Ye violets tender,
  And sweet roses bright,
Gay Lent lilies blending
  With pure lilies white.

Sweep, tides of rich music,
  The full veins along,
And pour in full measure,
  Sweet voices, your song.

Sing, sing, for He liveth,
   He lives as He said;
The Lord has arisen
   Unharm'd from the dead.

Clap, clap your hands, mountains;
   Ye valleys, resound;
Leap, leap for joy, fountains,
   Ye hills, catch the sound.
All triumph! He liveth!
   He lives, as He said;
The Lord has arisen
   Unharm'd from the dead!

SING THE BATTLE SHARP AND GLORIOUS.

SING the battle sharp and glorious,
   Sing the triumph won;
Life o'er death is now victorious,
   New things are begun.
Lay thy crown of pow'r aside,
   Death! thyself at length hast died:
      Alleluia! Alleluia!
   Christus resurrexit, Christus resurrexit.

Strong thou wert, and all around thee
  Men did bow to thee;
But the stronger Arm has found thee,
  Christ has set us free:
Forward, then, our King to see!
    Christ is gone to Galilee!
      Alleluia! Alleluia!
    Resurrexit vere, Resurrexit vere.

Up! and tell the soul so weary,
  Raise thy drooping head;
Christ has risen—truly risen—
  Risen, as He said.
Rise, and go your Lord to see!
    Hasten on to Galilee.
      Alleluia! Alleluia!
    Illic est videndus, Illic est videndus.

MARY TO THE SAVIOUR'S TOMB.

MARY to the Saviour's tomb
  Hasted at the early dawn;
Spice she brought and sweet perfume,
  But the Lord she loved had gone:

For awhile she lingering stood,
　　Filled with sorrow and surprise,
Trembling, while a crystal flood
　　Issued from her weeping eyes.

But her sorrows quickly fled
　　When she heard His welcome voice—
Christ has risen from the dead;
　　Now He bids her heart rejoice.
What a change His word can make,
　　Turning darkness into day!
Ye who weep for Jesus' sake,
　　He will wipe your tears away.

John Newton

HARK! THE HERALD ANGELS SING.

HARK! the herald angels sing
　　Glory to the new-born King,
Peace on earth, and mercy mild,
God and sinners reconciled.
Joyful all ye nations rise,
Join the triumph of the skies;

With the angelic host proclaim
Christ is born in Bethlehem.
Chorus.—Hark ! the herald angels sing
Glory to the new-born King.

Christ, by highest heaven adored—
Christ, the everlasting Lord ;
Late in time behold Him come,
Offspring of a Virgin's womb.
Veiled in flesh the Godhead see !
Hail the Incarnate Deity !
Pleased as Man with man to dwell,
Jesus, our Emmanuel.
        Chorus.—Hark ! etc.

Hail, the heaven-born Prince of Peace !
Hail, the Sun of Righteousness !
Light and life to all He brings,
Risen with healing in His wings.
Mild He lays His glory by—
Born that man no more may die ;
Born to raise the sons of earth ;
Born to give them second birth.
        Chorus.—Hark ! etc.
                Amen.

JESUS CHRIST IS RISEN.

ESUS CHRIST is risen to-day, Alleluia!
Alleluia!
Our triumphant holy-day, Alleluia! Alleluia!
Who did once upon the cross Alleluia! Alleluia!
Suffer to redeem our loss. Alleluia! Alleluia!

This, the Easter holy-day, Alleluia! etc.
Christians, haste your vows to pay;
Offer ye your praises; meet
At the Paschal Victim's feet.

Hymns of praise, then, let us sing Alleluia, etc.
Unto Christ, our heavenly King:
Who endured the cross and grave,
Sinners to redeem and save.

But the pains which He endured Alleluia, etc.
Our salvation has procured;
Now above the sky He's King,
Where the angels ever sing.

Say, O wond'ring Mary, say Alleluia, etc.
What thou sawest on thy way.
" I beheld, where Christ had lain,
Empty tomb and angels twain."

Christ, who once for sinners bled   Alleluia ! etc.
Now the first-born from the dead,
Throned in endless might and power,
Lives and reigns for evermore.

Hail, eternal hope on high !   Alleluia ! etc.
Hail, Thou King of victory !
Hail, Thou Prince of life adored !
Help and save us, gracious Lord !

Sing we to one God above   Alleluia ! etc.
Praise eternal as His love ;
Praise Him, all ye heavenly host,
Father, Son, and Holy Ghost.

WHITSUNTIDE.

INVOCATION TO THE HOLY GHOST.

COME, Holy Ghost ! Creator blest !
And in our souls take up Thy rest ;
Come with Thy grace and heavenly aid,
And fill the hearts which Thou hast made.

Praise we the Father and the Son,
And Holy Spirit with them One;
And may the Son on us bestow
The gifts that from the Spirit flow. Amen.

COME, HOLY GHOST

COME, Holy Ghost, who ever One
 Art with the Father and the Son;
Come, Holy Ghost, our souls possess,
With Thy full flood of holiness.

Let mouth, and heart, and flesh combine
To herald forth our creed divine,
And love so wrap our mortal frame
Others may catch the living flame.

Praise to the Father, with the Son,
And Holy Spirit, Three in One;
As ever was in ages past,
And shall be so while ages last.

CORPUS CHRISTI.

HYMN IN HONOR OF THE BLESSED SACRAMENT.

LAUDA Sion Salvatorem,
   Lauda Ducem et Pastorem,
     In hymnis et canticis,
Quantum potes tantum aude;
Quia major omni laude,
     Nec laudare sufficis.

Laudis thema specialis,
Panis vivus et vitalis
     Hodie proponitur,
Quem in sacræ mensa cœnæ
Turbæ fratrum duodenæ
     Datum non ambigitur.

Sit laus plena, sit sonora,
Sit jucunda, sit decora
     Mentis jubilatio,
Dies enim solemnis agitur,
In qua mensæ prima recolitur,
     Hujus institutio.

In hac mensa novi Regis,
Novum pascha novæ legis,
   hase vetus terminat,
Vetus tatem novitas,
Umbram fugat veritas,
   Noctem lux eliminat

Quod in cœna Christus gessit,
Faciendum hoc expressit
   In sui memoriam,
Docti sacris institutis,
Panem, vinem, in salutis
   Consecramus hostiam.

Dogma datur Christianis,
Quod in carnem transit panis,
   Et vinum in sanguinem,
Quod non capis, quod non vides,
Animosa firmat fides,
   Præter rerum ordinem.

Sub diversis speciebus,
Signis tantum et non rebus,
   Latent res eximiæ,

Hymns and Songs

Caro cibus sanguis potus :
Manet tamen Christus totus
    Sub utraque specie.

A sumente non concisus,
Non confractus, non divisus
    Integer accipitur.
Sumit unus, sumunt mille
Quantum isti, tantum ille,
    Nec sumptus consumitur.

Sumunt boni, sumunt mali ;
Sorte tamen inæquali,
    Vitæ vel interitus
Mors est malis, vita bonis,
Vide paris sumptionis
    Quam sit dispar exitus.

Fracto demum Sacramento,
Ne vacilles, sed memento,
Tantum esse sub fragmento,
    Quantum toto tegitur.
Nulla rei fit scissura :
Signi tantum fit fractura :
Qua nec status nec statura
    Signati minuitur.

Ecce panis angelorum,
Factus cibus viatorum :
Vere panis filiorum,
    Non mittendus canibus.
In figuris præsignatur,
Cum Isaac immolatur :
Agnus paschæ deputatur :
    Datur manna patribus.

Bone Pastor, panis vere
Jesu nostri miserere
    In terra viventium.
Tu nos pasce, nos tuere ;
Tu nos bona fac videre
    In terra viventium.

Tu qui cuncta scis et vales,
Qui nos pascis hic mortales ;
Tuos ibi commensales,
Cohæredes et sodales
    Fac sanctorum civium.
              Amen.

WHEN THE LOVING SHEPHERD.

WHEN the loving Shepherd,
   Ere He left the earth,
Shed, to pay our ransom,
   Blood of priceless worth,
These His lambs so cherished,
   Purchased for His own,
He would not abandon
   In the world alone.

Ere He makes us partners
   Of His realm on high,
Happy and immortal
   With Him in the sky,
Love immense, stupendous,
   Makes Him here below
Partner of our exile
   In this world of woe.

Lest one heart that loves him
   E'er should sigh with pain,
Pining for His presence,
   Seeking Him in vain,

He on earth would tarry,
　Near to every one,
That each heart might find Him
　On His altar-throne.

Jesus, food of angels,
　Monarch of the heart,
Oh ! that I could never
　From Thy face depart !
Yes, Thou ever dwellest
　Here for love of me ;
Hidden Thou remainest
　God of majesty.

Soon I hope to see Thee
　And enjoy Thy love
Face to face, sweet Jesus,
　In Thy heaven above.
But, on earth an exile,
　My delight shall be
Ever to be near Thee,
　Veiled for love of me.　Amen

JESUS, MY LORD.

JESUS, my Lord, my God, my All,
   How can I love Thee as I ought?
And how revere this wondrous gift,
   So far surpassing hope or thought?
Chorus.—Sweet Sacrament, we Thee adore ;
      Oh ! make us love Thee more and more.

Had I but Mary's sinless heart
   To love Thee with, my dearest King,
Oh ! with what bursts of fervent praise
   Thy goodness, Jesus, would I sing !
      Chorus.—Sweet Sacrament, etc.

Oh ! see upon the altar placed
   The Victim of divinest love.
Let all the earth below adore,
   And join the choirs of heaven above.
      Chorus.—Sweet Sacrament, etc.

Jesu, dear Pastor of the flock,
   We crowd in love about Thy feet.
Our voices yearn to praise Thee, Lord,
   And joyfully Thy presence greet.
      Chorus.—Sweet Sacrament, etc.

Sound, sound His praises higher still,
   And come, ye angels, to our aid.
'Tis God, 'tis God, the very God,
   Whose power hath men and angels made.
      Chorus.—Sweet Sacrament, etc.

Here Thou art come, O precious Gift!
   Our solace and our joy to be.
Increase the faith of loving hearts
   Who truly do believe in Thee.
      Chorus.—Sweet Sacrament, etc.

BLESSED BE THE LOVE OF JESUS.

BLESSED be the love of Jesus,
   Giving us His flesh and blood!
Blessed be His Mother Mary!
   Mother ever kind and good.

Blessed be the great St. Joseph!
   Sing, then, with devotion true,
" Dearest Jesus, Mary, Joseph,
   Heart and life I give to you."

BEHOLD THE LAMB!

BEHOLD the Lamb!
  O Thou for sinners slain!
Let it not be in vain
  That Thou hast died.
Thee for my Saviour let me take,
Thee, Thee alone my refuge make,
  Thy piercèd side.

Behold the Lamb!
  Into the sacred flood
Of Thy most precious blood
  My soul I cast.
Wash me and make me pure and clean,
Uphold me through life's changeful scene
  Till all be past.

Behold the Lamb!
  Archangels, fold your wings;
Seraphs, hush all the strings
  Of million lyres.
The Victim, veiled on earth, in love
Unveiled, enthroned, adored above,
  All heaven admires.

Behold the Lamb !
Drop down, ye glorious skies ;
He dies, He dies, He dies,
   For man once lost.
Yet, lo ! He lives, He lives, He lives,
And to His Church Himself He gives,
   Incarnate Host.

Behold the Lamb !
All hail ! Eternal Word,
Thou universal Lord,
   Purge out our leaven,
Clothe us with godliness and good,
Feed us with Thy celestial food,
   Manna from heaven.

Behold the Lamb !
Saints wrapped in blissful rest,
Souls waiting to be blessed,
   O Lord ! how long !
Thou, Church on earth, o'erwhelmed with
      fears,
Still in this vale of woe and tears
   Swell the full song.

Behold the Lamb!
Worthy is He alone
To sit upon the throne
Of God above.
One with the Ancient of all Days,
One with the Paraclete in praise,
All light, all love.

M. Bridges

HAIL, THOU LIVING BREAD!

HAIL, Thou Living Bread from heaven!
   Sacrament of awful might!
I adore Thee—I adore Thee—
Every moment, day and night.

Holiest Jesu!—Heart of Mary!
   O'er me shed your gifts divine:
Holiest Jesu! my Redeemer!
   All my heart and soul are Thine.

PRAISES OF THE BLESSED SACRAMENT.

VAULT of heaven, clear and bright
All spangled o'er with stars to-night,
Canst say how many worlds of light
Adorn thy glorious firmament?
Chorus.—For here I long my voice to raise
To Him who hath my heart always,
And fain would know how oft to praise
The sweet, All Holy Sacrament.

O shining sun! for every ray
That from thee beamed since Eden's day,
And shall, till this world pass away,
And all thy light and heat be spent:
Chorus.—For each bright ray my voice I'd raise
To Him who hath my heart always,
And sing a canticle of praise
To this Most Holy Sacrament.

O trackless sea! could I but save
And count each short-lived glist'ning wave;
Their sum would tell how oft I crave
To praise the Blessed Sacrament.

Hymns and Songs

Chorus.—O fields! for every grassy blade
    Of which thy beauteous robe is made,
    Let offerings sweet of praise be laid
      Before the Blessed Sacrament.

O pleasant gardens! could I know
How many flowers within you grow,
So many flowers of praise I'd strew
   Before the Blessed Sacrament.
Chorus.—O wide, wide world! canst tell to me
    How many grains of dust in thee?
    So many would my praises be
      T this Most Holy Sacrament.

O earth! thy praises have an end;
To seraphs I the task commend.
Their tireless voices they must lend
   To praise the Blessed Sacrament.
Chorus.—Eternity! duration long!
    To thee alone it doth belong
    To measure when should cease the
      song
      That lauds the Blessed Sacrament!

THE MOST HOLY SACRIFICE.

WHEN the Patriarch was returning,
   Crown'd with triumph, from the fray,
Him the peaceful king of Salem
   Came to meet upon his way:
Meekly bearing bread and wine,
Holy Priesthood's awful sign!

On the truth thus dimly shadow'd
   Later days a lustre shed;
When the great High-Priest eternal—
   Under forms of wine and bread—
For the world's immortal food
Gave His Flesh and gave His Blood.

Wondrous gift! The Word who moulded
   All things by His might divine,
Bread into His Body changes,
   Into His own Blood the wine—
What though sense no change perceives?
Faith admires, adores, believes!

He who once to die a Victim
   On the Cross did not refuse:
Day by day, upon our altars,
   That same Sacrifice renews;

Through His holy Priesthood's hands—
Faithful to His last commands!

While the people all uniting
  In the Sacrifice sublime,
Offer Christ to His high Father,
  Offer up themselves with Him;
Then together with the priest
On the living Victim feast! Amen.

AS PANTS THE HART FOR COOLING STREAMS.

AS pants the hart for cooling streams
  When heated in the chase;
So longs my soul, O God, for Thee,
  And Thy refreshing grace.

For Thee, my God—the living God—
  My thirsty soul doth pine:
Oh! when shall I behold Thy face,
  Thou Majesty Divine?

Why restless, why cast down, my soul?
  Hope still, and thou shalt sing
The praise of Him who is thy God—
  Thy health's eternal Spring.

To Father, Son, and Holy Ghost,
The God whom we adore,
Be glory as it was, is now,
And shall be evermore. Amen.

JESUS, JESUS, COME TO ME.

JESUS, Jesus, come to me.
  Oh! how much I long for Thee!
Come Thou, of all friends the best,
Take possession of my breast.
Chorus.—Comfort my poor soul distress'd,
  Take possession of my breast;
  Oh! how oft I sigh for Thee—
  Jesus, Jesus, come to me.

Empty is all worldly joy,
Ever mixed with some alloy;
Give me, my true Sov'reign good,
Jesus, Thy own Flesh and Blood.
  Chorus.—Comfort my poor soul, etc.

On the Cross three hours for me
Thou didst hang in agony;

I my heart to Thee resign;
Oh! what rapture to be Thine!
 Chorus.—Comfort my poor soul, etc.
         Amen.

O JESUS CHRIST, REMEMBER.

O JESUS CHRIST, remember,
 When Thou shalt come again,
Upon the clouds of heaven,
 With all Thy shining train—
When every eye shall see Thee
 In Deity reveal'd,
Who now upon this altar
 In silence art conceal'd—

Remember then, O Saviour,
 I supplicate of Thee,
That here I bow'd before Thee,
 Upon my bended knee;
That here I own'd Thy Presence,
 And did not Thee deny,
And glorified Thy greatness,
 Though hid from human eye.

Accept, divine Redeemer,
  The homage of my praise;
Be Thou the lignt and honor
  And glory of my days;
Be Thou my consolation
  When death is drawing nigh;
Be Thou my only treasure
  Through all eternity.

JESUS, GENTLEST SAVIOUR.

JESUS, gentlest Saviour,
  God of might and power,
Thou Thyself art dwelling
  In us at this hour;
Nature cannot hold Thee,
  Heaven is all too strait
For Thine endless glory
  And Thy royal state.

Out beyond the shining
  Of the farthest star,
Thou art ever stretching
  Infinitely far;

Yet the hearts of children
   Hold what worlds cannot,
And the God of wonders
   Loves the lowly spot.

As men to their gardens
   Go to seek sweet flowers,
In our hearts dear Jesus
   Seeks them at all hours.
Jesus, gentlest Saviour,
   Thou art in us now;
Fill us full of goodness
   Till our hearts o'erflow.

Pray the prayer within us
   That to heaven shall rise;
Sing the song that angels
   Sing above the skies.
Multiply our graces,
   Chiefly love and fear,
And, dear Lord, the chiefest,
   Grace to persevere.

Oh! how can we thank Thee
   For a gift like this—
Gift that truly maketh
   Heaven's eternal bliss?

Ah ! when wilt Thou always
  Make our hearts Thy home ?
We must wait for heaven ;
  Then the day will come.

Now at least we'll keep Thee
  All the time we may ;
But Thy grace and blessing
  We will keep alway.
When our hearts Thou leavest,
  Worthless though they be,
Give them to thy Mother,
  To be kept for Thee.

COMMUNION.

WHAT HAPPINESS CAN EQUAL MINE!

WHAT happiness can equal mine ?
  I've found the object of my love
My Saviour and my Lord divine
  Is come to me from heaven above.

He makes my heart His own abode,
   His flesh becomes my daily bread ;
He pours on me His healing blood,
   And with His life my soul is fed.

My Love is mine, and I am His ;
   In me He dwells, in Him I live ;
Where could I taste a purer bliss ?
   What greater boon could Jesus give ?

O royal banquet ! heavenly feast !
   O flowing Fount of life and grace !
Where God the giver, man the guest,
   Meet and unite in sweet embrace.

Dear Jesus, now my heart is Thine,
   Oh ! may it never from Thee fly ;
My God, be Thou for ever mine,
   And I Thine own eternally.

No more, O Satan ! thee I fear ;
   O world ! thy charms I now despise ;
For Christ Himself is with me here,
   My joy, my life, my Paradise !

Viva! viva Jesu

THE PRECIOUS BLOOD.

GLORY be to Jesus,
   Who in bitter pains
Poured for me His life-blood
   From His sacred veins !
Grace and life eternal
   In that blood I find ;
Blest be His compassion,
   Infinitely kind.

Blest through endless ages
   Be the precious stream
Which from endless torment
   Doth the world redeem.
There the fainting spirit
   Drinks of life her fill ;
There, as in a fountain,
   Laves herself at will.

O the blood of Christ !
   It soothes the Father's ire;
Opes the gates of heaven ;
   Quells eternal fire.

Hymns and Songs

Abel's blood for vengeance
   Pleaded to the skies ;
But the blood of Jesus
   For our pardon cries.

Oft as earth, exulting,
   Wafts its praise on high,
Hell with terror trembles,
   Heaven is filled with joy.
Lift ye, then, your voices ;
   Swell the mighty flood ;
Louder still and louder
   Praise the Precious Blood.

ROCK OF AGES.

ROCK of Ages, rent for me,
   Let me hide myself in Thee ;
Let the water and the blood,
From Thy riven side which flowed,
Be of sin the double cure :
Save from wrath, and make me pure.

Nothing in my hand I bring ;
Simply to Thy Cross I cling ;
Naked, come to Thee for dress ;
Helpless, look to Thee for grace ;
Foul, I to the fountain fly ;
Wash me, Saviour, or I die.

While I draw this fleeting breath,
When mine eyelids close in death,
When I soar to worlds unknown,
See Thee on Thy judgment-throne—
Rock of Ages, cleft for me,
Let me hide myself in Thee.

THE NAME OF JESUS.

ALL hail ! the power of Jesus' name !
    Let angels prostrate fall ;
Bring forth the royal diadem,
    And crown Him Lord of all !

Crown Him, ye martyrs of our God,
    Who from his altars call ;
Extol the stem of Jesse's rod,
    And crown Him Lord of all !

Let every kindred, every tribe,
  On this terrestrial ball,
To Him all majesty ascribe,
  And crown Him Lord of all!

Oh! that with yonder sacred throng
  We at His feet may fall!
We'll join the everlasting song,
  And crown Him Lord of all!

JESUS, THE VERY THOUGHT OF THEE.

JESUS, the very thought of Thee
  With sweetness fills my breast;
But sweeter far Thy face to see,
  And in Thy presence rest.

Nor voice can sing, nor heart can frame,
  Nor can the memory find
A sweeter sound than Thy blest name,
  O Saviour of mankind!

O hope of every contrite heart!
  O joy of all the meek!
To those who fall how kind Thou art!
  How good to those who seek!

But what to those who find? Ah! this
  Nor tongue nor pen can show.
The love of Jesus, what it is
  None but His loved ones know.

Jesu, our only joy be Thou,
  As Thou our prize wilt be.
Jesu, be Thou our glory now
  And through eternity.

MAY JESUS CHRIST BE PRAISED!

WHEN morning gilds the skies,
    My heart, awaking, cries,
        May Jesus Christ be praised!
Alike at work and prayer
To Jesus I repair,
        May Jesus Christ be praised!

The sacred minster-bell,
It peals o'er hill and dell,
        May Jesus Christ be praised!
Oh! hark to what it sings,
As joyously it rings,
        May Jesus Christ be praised!

When you begin the day,
Oh ! never fail to say,
    May Jesus Christ be praised !
And at your work rejoice
To sing with heart and voice,
    May Jesus Christ be praised !

Be this at meals your grace,
In every time and place,
    May Jesus Christ be praised !
Be this, when day is past,
Of all your thoughts the last,
    May Jesus Christ be praised !

To God the Word on high
The hosts of angels cry,
    May Jesus Christ be praised !
Let children too upraise
Their voice in hymns of praise,
    May Jesus Christ be praised !

Let earth's wide circle round
In joyful notes resound,
    May Jesus Christ be praised !
Let air, and sea, and sky
Through depth and height reply,
    May Jesus Christ be praised !

Caswall t,

JESUS SUBJECT TO HIS PARENTS.

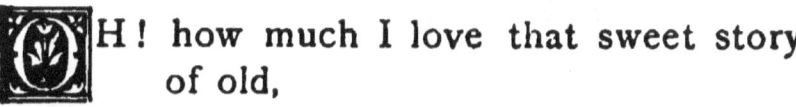H! how much I love that sweet story of old,
   Where Jesus is found 'mid the sages so gray!
And how very much do I love to be told
   Of all the wise things He so sweetly did say!

But oh! there is one part I love most to hear,
   Which tells me how Jesus, the Teacher of men,
His poor, humble parents so much did revere
   As to yield to their will and be subject to them.

They tell me this lesson was given for me
   That I might be docile, and willing, and mild,
And that my dear Jesus would have me to be
   An humble, a quiet and good little child.

Ah! then, I will strive to be gentle and good,
   For the sake of my Saviour, who loved me so dear.
I never again will be naughty or rude,
   But try to be all that my Jesus was here.

HEART OF THE HOLY CHILD.

HEART of the holy Child,
    Hide me in Thee;
Purest and undefiled,
    Purify me.
Joy of my infant life,
Far from evil passions rife,
Troubling this world of strife,
    Keep me with Thee.

Sweet Child of Bethlehem,
    Open Thine heart;
Lessons from Nazareth
    Deign to impart.
Mary and Joseph dear,
Let us be to Jesus near;
With you we shall not fear
    From Him to part.

INFANT JESUS, MEEK AND MILD.

INFANT Jesus, meek and mild,
    Look on me, a little child;
Pity mine and pity me,
Suffer me to come to Thee.

C Wesley

Heart of Jesus, I adore Thee,
Heart of Mary, I implore thee,
Heart of Joseph, pure and just—
In these hearts I put my trust. Amen.

SCHOOL HYMN.

 JESUS! God and man!
   For love of children once a
     child;
O Jesus! God and man!
We hail Thee, Saviour, sweet and mild.

O Jesus! God and man!
Make us poor children dear to Thee,
   And lead us to Thyself,
To love Thee for eternity.

O Jesus! Mary's Son!
On Thee for grace we children call;
   Make us all men to love,
But to love Thee beyond them all.

O Jesus! bless our work;
Our sorrows soothe, our sins forgive.
Oh! happy, happy they
Who in the Church of Jesus live!

O God most great and good!
At work or play, by night or day,
Make us remember Thee,
Who dost remember us alway.

F W Faber

FEAST OF ALL SOULS, NOVEMBER 2.

THE SOULS OF THE FAITHFUL.

YE souls of the faithful
    Who sleep in the Lord,
But as yet are shut out
    From your final reward,
Oh! would I could lend you
    Assistance to fly
From your prison below
    To your palace on high!

for Catholic Children.

O Father of mercies !
   Thine anger withhold ;
These works of Thy hand
   In Thy mercy behold.
Too oft from Thy path
   They have wandered aside ;
But Thee, their Creator,
   They never denied.

O tender Redeemer !
   Their misery see.
Deliver the souls
   That were ransomed by Thee.
Behold how they love Thee
   Despite of their pain !
Restore them, restore them
   To favor again.

O Spirit of grace !
   O consoler divine !
See how for Thy presence
   They longingly pine.
Oh ! then, to enliven
   Their sadness descend,
And fill them with peace
   And with joy in the end.

Hymns and Songs

O Mother of mercy!
   Dear Soother in grief!
Send thou to their torments
   A balmy relief,
Attemper the rigor
   Of justice severe,
And soften their flames
   With a pitying tear.

Ye patrons who watched
   O'er their safety below,
Oh! think how they need
   Your fidelity now;
And stir all the angels
   And saints of the sky
To plead for the souls
   That upon you rely.

Ye friends who, once sharing
   Their pleasures and pain,
Now haply ready,
   In Paradise reign,
Oh! comfort their hearts
   With a whisper of love,
And call them to share
   In your pleasures above.

O Fountain of goodness!
  Accept our sighs.
Let Thy mercy bestow
  What Thy justice denies.
So may Thy poor captives,
  Released from their woes,
Thy praises proclaim
  While eternity flows.

All ye who would honor
  The saints and their Head,
Remember, remember,
  To pray for the dead;
And they in return,
  From their misery freed,
To you will be friends
  In the hour of need. Amen.

OH! TURN TO JESUS, MOTHER, TURN.

H! turn to Jesus, Mother, turn,
  And call Him by His tend'rest
    names;
Pray for the holy souls that burn
  This hour amid the cleansing flames.

Hymns and Songs

Ah! they have fought a gallant fight.
  In death's cold arms they persevered;
And, after life's uncheery night,
  The harbor of their rest is neared.

Spouses of Christ they are; for He
  Was wedded to them by His blood;
And angels o'er their destiny
  In wondering adoration brood.

They are the children of thy tears;
  Then hasten, Mother, to their aid.
In pity think each hour appears
  An age while glory is delayed.

O Mary! let thy Son no more
  His lingering spouses thus expect;
God's children to their God restore,
  And to the Spirit His elect.

Pray, then, as Thou hast ever prayed;
  Angels and souls all look to thee;
God waits thy prayers, for He hath made
  Those prayers His law of charity.

FW Faber

HYMNS FOR FESTIVALS OF THE BLESSED VIRGIN MARY.

IMMACULATE CONCEPTION.

O PUREST OF CREATURES!

PART I.

 PUREST of creatures! sweet Mother, sweet Maid,
The one spotless womb wherein Jesus was laid,
Dark night hath come down on us, Mother, and we
Look out for thy shining, sweet Star of the Sea.

Deep night hath come down on this rough-spoken world,
And the banners of darkness are boldly unfurled,
And the tempest-tossed Church, all her eyes are on thee;
They look to thy shining, sweet Star of the Sea.

He gazed on thy soul—it was spotless and fair;
The empire of sin it had never been there;

For none had e'er owned thee, dear Mother, but He,
He was won by thy clear shining, sweet Star of the Sea.

Earth gave Him one lodging, 'twas deep in thy breast;
And God found a home where the sinner finds rest.
His home and His hiding-place both were in thee,
And He shone in thy shining, sweet Star of the Sea.

Oh! blissful and calm was the wonderful rest
That thou gavest thy God in thy virginal breast.
For the heaven He left He found heaven in thee,
And He shone in thy shining, sweet Star of the Sea.

PART II.

To sinners what comfort, to angels what mirth,
That God found one creature unfallen on earth,

One spot where His Spirit untroubled could be,
The depths of thy shining, sweet Star of the
  Sea !

Oh! shine on us brighter than ever, then
  shine ;
For the greatest of honors, dear Mother, is
  thine.
" Conceived without sin " thy new title shall
  be,
Clear light from thy birth-spring, sweet Star
  of the Sea.

So worship we God in these rude latter days ;
So worship we Jesus our Love, when we praise
His wonderful grace in the gifts He gave thee,
The gift of clear shining, sweet Star of the Sea.

Deep night hath come down on us, Mother—
  deep night,
And we need more than ever the guide of thy
  light;
For the darker the night is, the brighter
  should be
Thy beautiful shining, sweet Star of the Sea.

F W Faber

O MARIA, SINE LABE CONCEPTA.

O MARIA, O Maria, sine labe concep
O Maria, O Maria, sine labe concept
Sine labe originali, sine labe concepta;
O Maria, O Maria, sine labe concepta.
    Ora pro nobis, O Maria!
    Ora pro nobis, O Maria!

O Maria, O Maria (as above).

NATIVITY OF B. V. M.

INFANT'S HYMN TO THE B. V. MARY.

LITTLE children, hail the morn
    That our infant queen was born;
Sweetest flowers her crib adorn,
    Hail, sweet, happy morn!
Yes, she comes, the Morning Star,
Prophets hailed her from afar,
Heaven with earth no more at war,
    Hail, sweet, happy morn!

In the cradle Mary lies;
Angels see with glad surprise
Heaven reflected in her eyes,
  Hail, sweet, happy morn!
By thy sweet nativity,
By thy spotless infancy,
Infant queen, let infants be
  Ever dear to thee.

THE ANNUNCIATION.

HAIL, OCEAN STAR.

HAIL, Ocean Star!
  Dear Mother of my God!
Hail! O thou Virgin evermore,
Of Paradise the blissful door;
  Hail, Mary, hail!

Oh! by thy joy,
When Gabriel hailed thee blest,
In peace confirm us, one and all,
And make amends for Eva's fall;
  Hail, Mary, hail!

Break thou the chain
Of those whom sin has bound ;
Upon the blind thy radiance pour ;
Each ill remove, each bliss implore ;
    Hail, Mary, hail !

Show, show thyself
The Mother that thou art ;
Present our prayers before His throne,
Who for our sake became thy Son ;
    Hail, Mary, hail !

O Virgin blest !
O meekest of the meek !
Keep us in virtue's path secure ;
Keep us, oh ! keep us meek and pure ;
    Hail, Mary, hail !

Be thou our guide
Of all our life, we pray ;
Till, near thee, safe at last we rest,
With Christ's eternal vision blest ;
    Hail, Mary, hail !

Through every time,
Through all eternity,

for Catholic Children. 115

To Thee, O Father, Thee, O Son,
And Thee, O Spirit, Three in One !
    One glory be !

THE MAGNIFICAT.

MAGNIFICAT ! Inspired word,
    From Mary's raptured bosom poured,
My soul with Mary bless the Lord.
        Magnificat !

Magnificat ! Oh ! whence is this,
That God should heed my littleness ?
Henceforward all my name shall bless.
        Magnificat !

Magnificat ! Praise God alone,
The mercy of my Saviour own ;
For He hath mighty wonders done.
        Magnificat !

Magnificat ! His wondrous grace
Is manifest from race to race
Of them who fear before His face.
        Magnificat !

Magnificat! He hath brought down
The proud man from his lofty throne,
And lifted up the humble one.
    Magnificat!

Magnificat! Grace for the poor!
The poor who plead at Mercy's door;
The scornful rich shall have no more.
    Magnificat!

Magnificat! In me behold
Fulfilled the promises of old
To Abr'ham and the Fathers told.
    Magnificat!

Magnificat! The song of praise
To Father, Son, and Spirit raise!
One God throughout eternal days!
    Magnificat!

PURIFICATION.

JOY, JOY, THE MOTHER COMES.

JOY, joy, the Mother comes,
    And in her arms she brings
The Light of all the world,
    The Christ, the King of kings;
And in her heart the while
    All silently she sings.

Saint Joseph follows near,
    In rapture lost and love,
While angels round about
    In glowing circles move,
And o'er the Mother broods
    The everlasting Dove.

There in the temple court
    Old Simeon's heart beats high,
And Anna feeds her soul
    With food of prophecy;
But see, the shadows pass,
    The world's true Light draws nigh.

O Infant God, O Christ,
   O Light most beautiful,
Thou comest, Joy of joys,
   All darkness to annul,
And brightest lights of earth
   Beside Thy Light are dull.

                F. W. Faber.

ASSUMPTION.

SING, SING, YE ANGEL BANDS.

SING, sing, ye angel bands,
   All beautiful and bright;
For higher still, and higher,
   Through fields of starry light,
Your Virgin Queen ascends,
   Like the sweet moon at night.

O happy angels! look,
   How beautiful she is!
See! Jesus bears her up!
   Her hands are locked in His.
Oh! who can tell the height
   Of that fair Mother's bliss?

On through the countless stars
  Proceeds the bright array;
And Love Divine comes forth
  To light her on the way,
Through gloom of earthly night,
  Into celestial day.

Swifter and swifter grows
  That wondrous flight of love,
As though her heart were drawn
  More veh'mently above;
While joyful angels part
  A pathway for the Dove.

Hark! hark! through highest heaven
  What sounds of mystic mirth!
Mary, by God proclaimed
  The Queen of spotless birth,
And diademed with stars
  The lowliest of the earth.

And shall I lose thee then—
  Lose my sweet right to thee?
Oh! no; the Angels' Queen
  Man's Mother still will be;
And thou upon thy throne
  Wilt keep thy love for me.

F. W. Faber

HAIL, VIRGIN OF VIRGINS.

HAIL, Virgin of virgins !
   Thy praises we sing,
Thy throne is in heaven,
   Thy Son is its King.
The saints and the angels
   Thy glory proclaim ;
All nations devoutly
   Bow down at thy name.

Let all sing of Mary,
   The Mystical Rod,
The Mirror of Justice,
   The Handmaid of God.
Let valley and mountain
   Unite in her praise,
The sea with its waters,
   The sun with its rays.

Let souls that are holy
   Still holier be,
To sing with the angels,
   Sweet Mary, of thee.

for Catholic Children.

Let all who are sinners
   To virtue return,
That hearts without number
   With thy love may burn.

Thy name is our power,
   Thy love is our light;
We praise thee at morning,
   At noon, and at night.
We thank thee, we bless thee,
   When happy and free;
When tempted by Satan,
   We call upon thee.

Oh! be thou our Mother,
   And pray to the Lord,
That all may acknowledge
   And worship His word.
That good men with courage
   May walk in His ways,
And bad men, converted,
   May join in His praise.

STAR OF JACOB.

STAR of Jacob, ever beaming,
   Bright and clear, of peace the sign;
'Mid the stars of highest heaven
   Glows no purer ray than Thine.

All in stoles of snowy brightness,
   Unto Thee the angels sing;
Unto Thee the Virgin choirs—
   Mother of th' Eternal King!

Joyful in Thy path they scatter
   Roses white and lilies fair;
Yet with Thy chaste bosom's whiteness,
   Rose nor lily can compare.

Oh! that this low earth of ours,
   Answering th' angelic strain,
With Thy praises might re-echo,
   Till the heavens replied again.

Honor, glory, virtue, merit,
   Be to Thee, O Virgin's Son!
With the Father and the Spirit,
   While eternal ages run.

MONTH OF MARY.

SNOW and rain have vanished,
  Winds have ceased to wail,
Winter now is banished,
  Bright are hill and vale.
    Gentle Mother, hear us
      At thy altar pray;
    Queen of Virgins, bless us
      On this sweet May day.

Spring hath come with flowers,
  Spring hath come with light;
Soft and rosy hours
  Fill the day and night.
    Gentle Mother, etc.

Stars above us gleaming
  Tell of Mary's worth;
Blossoms round us teeming
  Speak her praise on earth.
    Gentle Mother, etc.

Grace, as to none other,
  To her soul was given;
She became the Mother
  Of the King of Heaven.
    Gentle Mother, etc.

God bestowed upon her
　Glories all her own;
Earth's sublimest honor,
　Heaven's queenly throne.
　　Gentle Mother, etc.

THE JOYOUS BIRDS ARE SINGING.

THE joyous birds are singing
　To welcome in the day;
The fairest buds are springing
　To hail the beauteous May.
While yet the morn is new,
　Come, maidens, to the bowers,
Before the falling dew
　Has dried upon the flowers.

Quick, cull the early roses
　In all their glowing bloom;
The jasmine which discloses
　Its fragrant, rich perfume.
With all the buds of spring
　Your blushing garlands twine,
And haste your wreaths to bring
　To deck Our Lady's shrine.

O thou whose home of splendor
  Is in yon starry skies!
The homage which we tender
  Receive with pitying eyes.
And from thy cloudless sphere
  Of never-dying day
Look on thy children here
  Who now before thee pray.

OH! BALMY AND BRIGHT.

OH! balmy and bright as a moonlit night
  Is the love of our blessed Mother;
    It lies like a beam
    Over life's cold stream,
And life knows not such another.

The month of May with a grace a day
  Shines bright with our blessed Mother,
    The angels on high
    In the glorious sky,
Oh! they know not such another.

The angels' Queen, the beautiful Queen,
　Is the sinner's patient Mother;
　　With pardon and peace,
　　And the soul's release,
Oh! we know not such another.

O Mary's heart, th' immaculate heart,
　The heart of the Saviour's Mother!
　　All heaven shows bright
　　In its dear, sweet light;
God hath not made such another!

Ave maris Stella

HAIL! BRIGHT STAR OF OCEAN.

HAIL! bright Star of Ocean,
　God's own Mother blest,
Ever-sinless Virgin,
　Gate of heavenly rest.

Taking that sweet Ave
　Which from Gabriel came,
Peace confirm within us,
　Changing Eva's name.

Break the captive's fetters;
  Light on blindness pour;
All our ills expelling,
  Every bliss implore.

Show thyself a mother;
  May the Word divine,
Born for us thine Infant,
  Hear our prayers through thine.

Virgin all excelling,
  Mildest of the mild,
Freed from guilt, preserve us
  Meek and undefiled.

Keep our life all spotless,
  Make our way secure,
Till we find in Jesus
  Joy for evermore.

Through the highest heaven,
  To the Almighty Three,
Father, Son, and Spirit,
  One same glory be.

Caswall T, 1846.

STAR OF THE OCEAN, HAIL!

STAR of the Ocean, hail!
   Mother of God on high,
And Virgin evermore,
   Blest Portal of the sky.

Oh! think on Gabriel's voice
   From whom that Ave came,
And stablish us in peace,
   Reversing Eva's name.

Loosen the sinner's bands,
   All evils drive away;
Bring light unto the blind,
   And for all graces pray.

Exert a Mother's sway,
   It is the suppliant's plea,
With Him who, born for us,
   Deigned to be born of thee.

O pure, O spotless Maid!
   Whose meekness all surpassed,
Our lusts and passions quell,
   And make us meek and chaste.

Preserve our lives unstained,
   And guard us on our way;
Until we come to thee,
   To joys that ne'er decay.

Praise to the Father be,
   With Christ, His Only Son,
And to the Holy Ghost,
   Thrice blessed Three in One.

MAIDEN MOTHER, MEEK AND MILD.

MAIDEN Mother, meek and mild,
   Take, oh! take me for thy child.
All my life, oh! let it be
My best joy to think of thee,
My best joy to think of thee.

When my eyes are closed in sleep,
Through the night my slumbers keep;
Make my latest thought to be
How to love thy Son and thee,
How to love thy Son and thee.

Teach me, when the sunbeam bright
Calls me with its golden light,
How my waking thoughts may be
Turned to Jesus and to thee,
Turned to Jesus and to thee.

And, oh ! teach me through the day
Oft to raise my heart and say,
" Maiden Mother, meek and mild,
Guard, oh ! guard thy faithful child.
Guard, oh ! guard thy faithful child."

Thus, sweet Mother, day and night,
Thou shalt guide my steps aright;
And my dying words shall be,
" Virgin Mother, pray for me,
Virgin Mother, pray for me."   Amen.

MOTHER MARY, AT THINE ALTAR.

MOTHER Mary, at thine altar
    We thy loving children kneel;
With a faith that cannot falter,
    To thy goodness we appeal.

We are seeking for a mother
   O'er the earth so waste and wide ;
And from off the Cross our Brother
   Points to Mary by His side.

Thou wilt love us, thou wilt guide us
   With a mother's fondest care ;
And our Father, God above us,
   Bids us fly for refuge there.
Life's temptations are before us,
   We must mingle in the strife ;
If thy fondness watch not o'er us,
   All unsafe will be our life.

So we take thee for our Mother,
   And we claim our right to be,
By the gift of our dear Brother,
   Loving children unto thee ;
And our humble consecration
   Thou wilt surely not despise,
From thy high and lofty station
   Close to Jesus in the skies.

Mother Mary, to thy keeping
   We ourselves to thee confide,
Toiling, resting, waking, sleeping,
   To be ever at thy side.

Cares that vex us, joys that please us
Life and death we trust to thee:
Thou wilt make them all for Jesus,
And for all eternity.

F W Faber

MARY, MOTHER! SHIELD US.

MARY, Mother!
   Shield us through life!
Protect us from
   The ocean's strife.

Star of the Main,
   Beneath thy veil,
Clinging to thee,
   We safely sail.

O Mother dear!
   O Virgin blest!
Our footsteps guide
   Till death's long rest.

Sweet Morning Star,
   When life is o'er,
Then land us on
   The eternal shore. Amen.

THIS IS THE IMAGE OF THE QUEEN.

THIS is the image of the Queen
   Who reigns in bliss above;
Of her who is the hope of men,
   Whom men and angels love!
Most holy Mary, at thy feet
   I bend a suppliant knee;
Dear Mother of my God, I pray,
   Do thou remember me!

The sacred homage that we pay
   To Mary's image here,
To Mary's self at once ascends,
   Above the starry sphere.
Most holy Mary, at thy feet
   I bend a suppliant knee;
In all my joy, in all my pain,
   Do thou remember me!

How fair soever be the form
   Which here your eyes behold,
Its beauty is by Mary's self
   Excelled a thousand-fold.

Most holy Mary, at thy feet
  I bend a suppliant knee;
In my temptations each and all,
  Do thou remember me!

Sweet are the flow'rets we have culled
  This image to adorn;
But sweeter far is Mary's self,
  That rose without a thorn.
Most holy Mary, at thy feet
  I bend a suppliant knee;
When on the bed of death I lie,
  Do thou remember me.

O Lady! by the stars that make
  A glory round thy head;
And by thy pure uplifted hands,
  That for thy children plead;
When at the judgment-seat I stand,
  And my dread Saviour see;
When hell is raging for my soul,
  Oh! then remember me.

O MARY, MY MOTHER!

MARY, my Mother! most lovely, most mild,
Look down upon me, your weak, lowly child;
From the land of my exile I call upon thee;
Then Mary, my Mother, look kindly on me.

O Mary! in pity look down upon me;
'Tis the voice of thy child that is calling on thee.

If thou shouldst forsake me, ah! where shall I go?
My comfort and hope in this valley of woe;
When the world and its dangers with terror I view,
Sweet hopes come to cheer me in pointing to you.

O Mary! in pity look down upon me;
'Tis the voice of thy child that is calling on thee.

In sorrow, in darkness, be still at my side,
My light and my refuge, my guard and my guide;

Though snares should surround me, yet why
   should I fear?
I know I am weak, but my Mother is near;

Then, Mary, in pity, look down upon me;
'Tis the voice of thy child that is calling on
   thee.

DAILY, DAILY SING TO MARY.

DAILY, daily sing to Mary;
   Sing, my soul, her praises due;
All her feasts, her actions worship
   With the heart's devotion true.
Lost in wond'ring contemplation,
   Be her majesty confessed;
Call her Mother, call her Virgin—
   Happy Mother, Virgin blest!

She is mighty to deliver;
   Call her, trust her lovingly:
When the tempest rages round thee,
   She will calm the troubled sea.
Gifts of heaven she has given,
   Noble Lady, to our race;
She, the Queen, who decks her subjects
   With the light of God's own grace.

All my senses, heart, affections,
  Strive to sound her glory forth ;
Spread abroad the sweet memorials
  Of the Virgin's priceless worth.
Sing in songs of praise unending,
  Sing the world's majestic Queen ;
Weary not, nor faint in telling
  All the gifts she gives to men.

GENTLE STAR OF OCEAN.
Ave Maris Stella.

GENTLE Star of Ocean,
  Portal of the sky !
Ever Virgin Mother
  Of the Lord most High !
Oh ! by Gabriel's Ave,
  Uttered long ago,
Eva's name reversing,
  Stablish peace below.

Break the captive's fetters,
  Light on blindness pour ;
All our ills expelling,
  Every bliss implore.

Show thyself a Mother
  Offer Him our sighs,
Who for us Incarnate,
  Did not thee despise.

Virgin of all virgins,
  To thy shelter take us;
Gentlest of the gentle,
  Chaste and gentle make us.
Through the highest heaven,
  To th' Almighty Three,
Father, Son, and Spirit,
  One same glory be.

HAIL, QUEEN OF HEAVEN!

HAIL, Queen of Heaven, the Ocean Star
  Guide of the wand'rer here below!
Thrown on life's surge, we claim thy care,
  Save us from peril and from woe.
    Mother of Christ, Star of the Sea,
    Pray for the wand'rer, pray for me.

O gentle, chaste, and spotless Maid!
   We sinners make our prayers to thee;
Remind thy Son that He has paid
   The price of our iniquity.
      Virgin most pure, Star of the Sea,
      Pray for the sinner, pray for me.

Sojourners in this vale of tears,
   To thee, blest Advocate, we cry;
Pity our sorrows, calm our fears,
   And soothe with hope our misery.
      Refuge in grief, Star of the Sea,
      Pray for the mourner, pray for me.

And while to Him who reigns above,
   In Godhead One, in Persons Three,
The source of life, of grace, of love,
   Homage we pay on bended knee;
      Do thou, bright Queen, Star of the Sea,
      Pray for thy children, pray for me.

THE PILGRIM QUEEN OF MERRY ENGLAND.

THERE sat a Lady all on the ground,
　　Rays of the morning circled her round !
Save thee, and hail to thee, Gracious and Fair !
In the chill twilight what wouldst thou there?

" Here I sit desolate," sweetly said she,
" Though I'm a Queen, and my name is Marie:
Robbers have rifled my garden and store,
Foes they have stolen my Heir from my bower.

" They said they could keep him far better than I,
In a palace all His, planted deep and raised high,
'Twas a palace of ice, hard and cold as were they,
And, when summer came, it all melted away.

" Next they would barter Him, Him the Supreme,
For the spice of the desert and gold of the stream ;
And me they bid wander in weeds and alone,
In this green merry land which once was my own."

I looked on that Lady, and out from her eyes
Came the deep, glowing blue of Italy's skies;
And she raised up her head, and she smiled as
    a Queen
On the day of her crowning, so bland and
    serene.

"A moment," she said, "and the dead shall
    revive;
The giants are failing, the saints are alive;
I am coming to rescue my home and my reign,
And Peter and Paul are close in my train."

HAIL, VIRGIN! DEAREST MARY!

HAIL, Virgin! dearest Mary!
    Our lovely Queen of May!
O spotless, blessed Lady!
    Our lovely Queen of May!
Thy children humbly bending
    Around thy shrine so dear,
With heart and voice ascending,
    Sweet Mary, hear our prayers.
      Hail, Virgin! etc.

Behold earth's blossoms springing
  In beauteous form and hue ;
All nature gladly bringing
  Her sweetest charms to you.
We'll gather fresh, bright flowers
  To bind our fair Queen's brow;
From gay and verdant bowers
  We haste to crown thee now.
    Hail, Virgin ! etc.

The rose and lily wreathing,
  The humble violet fair,
To thee their perfumes breathing,
  With sweetness scent the air.
The mignonette, the lilac,
  And sweet forget-me-not,
The eglantine and myrtle,
  To grace your wreath we've brought.
    Hail, Virgin ! etc.

The heliotrope, sweet type of love,
  And star of Bethlehem, too,
The lily of the valley,
  Complete the wreath for you.

And now, our blessed Mother,
Smile on our festal day;
Accept our wreath of flowers,
And be our Queen of May.
Hail, Virgin! etc.

LITANY OF THE BLESSED VIRGIN.

Kyrie eleison,	Lord have mercy on us.
Kyrie eleison,	Lord have mercy on us.
Christe eleison,	Christ have mercy on us.
Christe eleison,	Christ have mercy on us.
Kyrie eleison,	Lord have mercy on us.
Kyrie eleison,	Lord have mercy on us.
Christe audi nos,	Christ hear us.
Christe exaudi nos,	Christ graciously hear us.
Pater de cœlis Deus,	God the Father of heaven,
Fili Redemptor mundi Deus,	God the Son, Redeemer of the world,
Spiritus Sancte Deus,	God the Holy Ghost,
Sancta Trinitas, unus Deus,	Holy Trinity, one God,

Miserere nobis. / *Have mercy on us.*

Sancta Maria,	Holy Mary,
Sancta Dei Genitrix,	Holy Mother of God,
Sancta Virgo Virginum,	Holy Virgin of Virgins,
Mater Christi,	Mother of Christ,
Mater divinæ gratiæ,	Mother of divine grace,
Mater purissima,	Mother most pure,
Mater castissima.	Mother most chaste,
Mater inviolata,	Mother inviolate,
Mater intemerata,	Mother undefiled,
Mater amabilis,	Mother most amiable,
Mater admirabilis,	Mother most admirable,
Mater Creatoris,	Mother of our Creator,
Mater Salvatoris,	Mother of our Saviour,
Virgo prudentissima,	Virgin most prudent,
Virgo veneranda,	Virgin most venerable,
Virgo prædicanda,	Virgin most renowned,
Virgo potens,	Virgin most powerful,
Virgo clemens,	Virgin most merciful,
Virgo fidelis,	Virgin most faithful,
Speculum justitiæ,	Mirror of justice,
Sedes sapientiæ,	Seat of wisdom,
Causa nostræ lætitiæ,	Cause of our joy,
Vas spirituale,	Spiritual vessel,
Vas honorabile,	Vessel of honor,
Vas insigne devotionis,	Singular vessel of devotion,
Rosa Mystica,	Mystical rose,

Ora pro nobis. — *Pray for us.*

Turris Davidica,	Tower of David,
Turris eburnea,	Tower of ivory,
Domus aurea,	House of gold,
Fœderis arca,	Ark of the covenant,
Janua Cœli,	Gate of heaven,
Stella matutina,	Morning star,
Salus infirmorum,	Health of the sick,
Refugium peccatorum,	Refuge of sinners,
Consolatrix afflictorum,	Comfort of the afflicted,
Auxilium Christianorum,	Help of Christians,
Regina Angelorum,	Queen of Angels,
Regina Patriarcharum,	Queen of Patriarchs,
Regina Prophetarum,	Queen of Prophets,
Regina Apostolorum,	Queen of Apostles,
Regina Martyrum,	Queen of Martyrs,
Regina Confessorum,	Queen of Confessors,
Regina Virginum,	Queen of Virgins,
Regina Sanctorum omnium,	Queen of all Saints,
Regina sine labe originali concepta,	Queen conceived without original sin.
Agnus Dei, qui tollis peccata mundi.	Lamb of God, who takest away the sins of the world.
Parce nobis Domine.	*Spare us, O Lord.*

Ora pro nobis. — *Pray for us.*

Agnus Dei, qui tollis pec- Lamb of God, who takest
cata mundi, away the sins of the
world,
Exaudi nos Domine. *Graciously hear us, O Lord.*
Agnus Dei, qui tollis pec- Lamb of God, who takest
cata mundi, away the sins of the
world,
Miserere nobis. *Have mercy on us.*
Christe audi nos. Christ hear us.
Christe exaudi nos. *Christ graciously hear us.*
V. Ora pro nobis, sancta *V.* Pray for us, O holy
Dei Genitrix. Mother of God.
R. Ut digni efficiamur pro- *R.* That we may be made
missionibus Christi. worthy of the promises
of Christ.
Amen.

THE SAINTS.

SAINT JOSEPH.

O HOLY Patron! thee saluting,
    Here we meet, with hearts sincere;
Blest Saint Joseph, all, uniting,
    Call on thee to hear our prayer.
Chorus.—Happy saint, in bliss adoring
        Jesus, Saviour of mankind,

Hear thy children thee imploring,
  May we thy protection find.

Worldly dangers for them fearing,
  Youthful hearts to thee we bring ;
Grant, in virtue persevering,
  Vice may ne'er their bosom sting.
    Chorus.—Happy saint, etc.

Thou who faithfully attended
  Him whom heaven and earth adore ;
Who with pious care defended
  Mary, Virgin ever pure.
    Chorus.—Happy saint, etc.

May our fervent prayers ascending,
  Move thee for our souls to plead ;
May thy smile of peace descending,
  Benedictions on us shed.
    Chorus—Happy saint, etc.

Through this life, oh ! watch around us,
  Fill with love our every breath,
And, when parting fear surrounds us,
  Guide us through the toils of death.
    Chorus.—Happy saint, etc.

THE PATRONAGE OF ST. JOSEPH.

EAR husband of Mary, dear nurse of her Child,
Life's ways are full weary, the desert is wild;
Bleak sands are all round us, no home can we see;
Sweet spouse of our Lady, we lean upon thee.

For thou to the pilgrim art father and guide,
And Jesus and Mary felt safe by thy side;
Ah blessed Saint Joseph! how safe should I be,
Sweet spouse of our Lady, if thou wert with me.

O blessed Saint Joseph! how great was thy worth,
The one chosen shadow of God upon earth!
The father of Jesus—ah! then, wilt thou be,
Sweet spouse of our Lady, a father to me?

When the treasures of God were unsheltered on earth,
Safe keeping was found for them both in thy worth;
O father of Jesus! be father to me,
Sweet spouse of our Lady, and I will love thee.

F W Faber

HAIL, HOLY JOSEPH.

HAIL, holy Joseph, hail!
  Chaste spouse of Mary, hail!
Pure as the lily-flower
  In Eden's peaceful vale.

Hail, holy Joseph, hail!
  Father of Christ esteemed;
Father be thou to those
  Thy Foster-Son redeemed.

Hail, holy Joseph, hail!
  Prince of the House of God;
May His best graces be
  By thy sweet hands bestowed.

Hail, holy Joseph, hail!
  Beloved of angels, hail!
Cheer thou the hearts that faint,
  And guide the steps that fail.

Hail, holy Joseph, hail!
  God's choice wert thou alone;
To thee the Word made flesh
  Was subject as a Son.

Hail, holy Joseph, hail!
  Teach us our, flesh to tame;
And, Mary, keep the hearts
  That love thy husband's name.

Mother of Jesus, bless,
  And bless, ye saints on high,
All meek and simple souls
  That to St. Joseph cry.

SAINT PAUL.

ALL ye who groan beneath
  A load of ills oppressed,
Entreat Saint Paul, and he will pray
  The Lord to give you rest.

Chorus.—O victim dear to heaven,
    O Paul, thou teacher true!
  Thou love and joy of Christendom,
    To thee for help we sue.

Pierced by the flame of love,
  Descending from on high,
'Twas thine to preach the faith which once
  Thou soughtest to destroy.
    Chorus.—O victim dear, etc.

Nor toil, nor threatened death,
  Nor tempest, scourge, or chain,
Could from the Assembly of the Saints
  Thy loving heart detain.
    Chorus.—O victim dear, etc.

Oh ! by that quenchless love
  Which burnt in thee of yore,
Take pity on our miseries;
  Our fainting hope restore.
    Chorus.—O victim dear, etc.

True Champion of the Lord !
  Crush thou the schemes of hell,
And with adoring multitudes
  The sacred temples fill.
    Chorus.—O victim dear, etc.

Through thy prevailing prayer
  May charity abound ;
Sweet charity which knows no ill,
  Which nothing can confound.
    Chorus.—O victim dear, etc.

Oh! for our country pray;
  Men's hearts have grown so cold;
Confused by doubts, afar they stray
  From Christ's true, sacred fold.
    Chorus.—O victim dear, etc.

Great Patron! pray for those
  Whom error has oppressed;
Oh! bring them all back home again
  To freedom, faith, and rest.
    Chorus.—O victim dear, etc.

Praise to the Father be;
  Praise to the Son who rose;
Praise to the Spirit Paraclete,
  While age on ages flows.
    Chorus.—O victim dear, etc.

ST. MARY MAGDALENE.

FROM the highest heights of glory,
    'Mid the sweets of endless calm,
Mary's spirit in its rapture
  On the earth is dropping balm.

On the bosom of the Saviour,
  Like a flower of stainless white,
Lies the trophy of His mercy,
  In a blaze of heavenly light.

And yet thou, too, once wert wandering,
  Once wert soiled with darkest stains,
Who art now the fairest blossom
  In the land where Jesus reigns.
Thou wert wretched, thou wert drooping,
  Thou wert crushed upon the earth,
Who art greater now, and grander
  Than an angel in his mirth.

Queen of penance ! Queen of fervor !
  Thou art martyr, too, of love,
And thy likeness to thy Saviour
  Makes the angels glad above.
Oh ! how wisely hast thou chosen
  For thyself the better part,
To be braided like a jewel
  On thy Saviour's sacred heart.

Still the fragrance of thine ointment
  All the earth is filling now ;

And thy tears are turned to jewels
   For a crown upon thy brow;
There are thousands in all ages
   Come to Christ because of thee.
Oh! then, Mary, with thy converts
   In thy kindness number me.

F W Faber

SAINT AGNES.

SAINT Agnes, holy child,
   All purity,
Oh! may we, undefiled,
   Be pure as thee;
Ready our blood to shed
   Rather than sin to wed,
And forth as martyrs led,
   To die like thee.

Chorus.—Saint Agnes, holy child,
   All purity,
Oh! may we, undefiled,
   Be pure as thee.

O gentle Patroness
   Of holy youth !
Ask God all those to bless
   Who love the truth ;
And guide us on our way
   To the eternal day,
With our hearts pure and gay,
   Dear saint, like thee.
Chorus.—Saint Agnes, holy child, etc.

Look down and hear our prayer
   From realms above,
Show us a sister's care,
   A mother's love ;
Be near us all through life,
   Till in eternal life,
Free from all care and strife,
   In heaven with thee.
Chorus.—Saint Agnes, holy child, etc.

LET THE DEEP ORGAN SWELL THE LAY.

(To St. Cæcilia.)

LET the deep organ swell the lay,
In honor of this festive day;
Let the harmonious choirs proclaim
Cæcilia's ever-blessed name.

Rome gave the virgin martyr birth,
Whose holy name hath filled the earth;
And from the early dawn of youth,
She fixed her heart on God and truth.

Then from the world's bewildering strife,
In peace she spent her holy life—
Teaching the organ to combine
With voice, to praise the Lamb divine.

Cæcilia, with a twofold crown
Adorned in heaven, we pray look down
Upon thy fervent votaries here,
And hearken to their humble prayer.

FIRST FLOWERET OF THE DESERT WILD.

(St. Rose of Lima.)

FIRST floweret of the desert wild!
   Whose leaves the sweets of grace
     exhale,
We greet thee, Lima's sainted child—
   Rose of America—all hail!

When first appeared the infant smile,
   Beaming upon thy features meek,
It seemed as if there blushed, the while,
   The Rose-bud on thy virgin cheek.

And hence thy name, St. Rose, was given,
   Not by thy earthly parents' choice,
But by the holy Queen of Heaven,
   Who bade thee in that name rejoice.

Transplanted from the worldly gaze,
   Which sometimes taints the fairest
     flowers,
In solitude thou lovedst to praise
   Thy Spouse amid Religion's bowers.

There oft thy mind, too pure, too high,
    For this low world of sin and strife,
Held blest communion with the sky,
    Enjoying heaven in mortal life.

And once, amid thy rapturous prayer,
    Thy heavenly Spouse himself came down
Most sweetly breathing in thine ear,
    ' Rose of my heart, receive thy crown."

And whilst amid His glories now,
    Thou seest me face to face—oh! deign,
St. Rose, to hear thy suppliants' vow,
    That grace and glory we may gain.

GUARDIAN ANGELS.

(Blest Spirits of Light.)

BLEST spirits of light! ye who have not
    forsaken
The children of earth, though fallen from
    bliss,
Oh! still watch around us; our bosoms awaken
    To thoughts of a world that is brighter than
    this.

Chorus.—Oh ! kindly watch o'er us, oh ! guard and protect us,
Sweet angels and guides to the mansions of bliss.

The lily of innocence fondly we'll cherish,
  Averting whatever its blossoms may stain.
And oh ! if 'tis fading and ready to perish,
  Restore it, sweet angel, to beauty again.
Chorus.—Oh ! kindly watch o'er us, etc.

Then pray for thy children, and guard and defend them,
  And ask of our Father, thy Maker, that we
May faithfully serve Him—may love and adore Him
  In heaven, sweet angel, united with thee.
Chorus.—Oh ! kindly watch o'er us, etc.

SWEET ANGEL OF MERCY.

SWEET Angel of Mercy !
  By Heaven's decree
Benignly appointed
  To watch over me !

Hymns and Songs

Without thy protection,
  So constant and nigh,
I could not well live;
  I should tremble to die!

All thanks for thy love,
  Dear companion and friend!
Oh! may it continue
  With me to the end.
Oh! cease not to keep me,
  Blest guide of my youth,
In the ways of religion
  And virtue and truth.

Support me in weakness;
  My spirit inflame;
Defend me in danger;
  Secure me from shame,
That, safe from temptation
  Or sudden surprise,
I may mount the straight path
  That ascends to the skies.

When I wander in error,
  My footsteps recall;

for Catholic Children.

Remove from my path
  What might cause me to fall;
Preserve me from sin;
  And in all that I do
May God and His glory
  Be ever in view.

O thou who didst witness
  My earliest breath!
Be with me, I pray,
  In the hour of my death;
Console me in sadness;
  Refresh me in pain;
And teach me how best
  I may mercy obtain;

That, cleansed by confession
  Complete and sincere,
From every defilement
  Afflicting me here,
All glowing with love,
  I may gladly depart,
With faith on my lips,
  And with hope in my heart!

Nor then do thou leave me,
  Angelical friend,
But at the tribunal
  Of Judgment attend,
And cease not to plead
  For my soul, till, forgiven,
Thou bear it aloft
  To the palace of heaven!

Caswall.

MISCELLANEOUS.

THE GOOD SHEPHERD.

I MET the Good Shepherd
  But now on the plain,
As homeward He carried
  His lost one again;
I marvelled how gently
  His burden He bore;
And as He passed by me
  I knelt to adore.

" O Shepherd, Good Shepherd!
  Thy wounds they are deep;

The wolves have sore hurt Thee,
  In helping Thy sheep;
Thy raiment all over
  With crimson is dyed;
And what is this rent
  They have made in Thy side?

"Ah me! how the thorns
  Have entangled thy hair;
And cruelly riven
  That forehead so fair!
How feebly Thou drawest
  Thy faltering breath!
And lo! on Thy face
  Is the shadow of death!

"O Shepherd, Good Shepherd
  And is it for me
This grievous affliction
  Has fallen on Thee?
Ah! then, let me strive,
  For the love Thou hast borne,
To give Thee no longer
  Occasion to mourn."

THE PILGRIMS OF THE NIGHT.

HARK, hark, my soul, angelic songs are swelling
O'er earth's green fields and ocean's wave-beat shore:
How sweet the truth those blessed strains are telling
Of that new life when sin shall be no more!
 Angels of Jesus, angels of light,
 Singing to welcome the pilgrims of the night.

Darker than night life's shadows fall around us,
And, like benighted men, we miss our mark;
God hides Himself, and grace hath scarcely found us,
'Ere Death finds out his victims in the dark.
 Angels of Jesus, etc.

Onward we go; for still we hear them singing,
"Come, weary souls; for Jesus bids you come;"
And through the dark its echoes sweetly ringing,
The music of the Gospel leads us home.
 Angels of Jesus, etc.

Rest comes at length ; though life be long and dreary,
  The day must dawn and darksome night be past ;
All journeys end in welcomes to the weary,
  And heaven, the heart's true home, will come at last.
      Angels of Jesus, etc.

Cheer up, my soul, Faith's moonbeams softly glisten
  Upon the breast of Life's most troubled sea ;
And it will cheer thy drooping heart to listen
  To those glad songs which angels mean for thee.
      Angels of Jesus, etc.

Angels, sing on, your faithful watches keeping ;
  Sing us sweet fragments of the songs above ;
While we toil on, and soothe ourselves with weeping,
  Till Life's long night shall break in endless love.
      Angels of Jesus, etc.

NEARER, MY GOD, TO THEE.

NEARER, my God, to Thee,
　　Nearer to Thee!
E'en though it be a cross
　　That raiseth me,
Still all my song shall be,
　　Nearer to Thee,
Nearer, my God, to Thee,
　　Nearer to Thee!

Though like the wanderer,
　　The sun gone down,
Darkness be over me,
　　My rest a stone,
Yet in my dreams
　　I'd be nearer to Thee,
Nearer, my God, to Thee,
　　Nearer to Thee!

There let the way appear
　　Steps unto heaven;
All that Thou sendest me
　　In mercy given;

Angels to beckon me,
  Nearer to Thee,
Nearer, my God, to Thee!
  Nearer to Thee!

Then with my waking thoughts
  Bright with Thy praise,
Out of my stony griefs
  Bethel I'll raise ;
So by my woes to be
  Nearer to Thee,
Nearer, my God, to Thee,
  Nearer to Thee!

Or if on joyful wing,
  Cleaving the sky,
Sun, moon, and stars forgot,
  Upward I fly,
Still all my song shall be,
  Nearer to Thee,
Nearer, my God, to Thee,
  Nearer to Thee!

O PARADISE!

O PARADISE! O Paradise!
   Who doth not crave for rest?
Who would not seek the happy land
   Where they that loved are blest?

O Paradise! O Paradise!
   The world is growing old:
Who would not be at rest and free
   Where love is never cold?

O Paradise! O Paradise!
   Wherefore doth death delay—
Bright death, that is the welcome dawn
   Of our eternal day?

O Paradise! O Paradise!
   'Tis weary waiting here:
I long to be where Jesus is,
   To feel, to see Him near.

O Paradise! O Paradise!
   I want to sin no more!
I want to be as pure on earth
   As on thy spotless shore.

O Paradise! O Paradise!
  I greatly long to see
The special place my dearest Lord
  Is furnishing for me.

O Paradise! O Paradise!
  I feel 'twill not be long:
Patience! I almost think I hear
  Faint fragments of thy song.

HEAVEN IS THE PRIZE.

YES, Heaven is the prize
  My soul shall strive to gain:
One glimpse of Paradise
  Repays a life of pain.
      'Tis Heaven; 'tis Heaven; yes,
        Heaven is the prize!
      'Tis Heaven; 'tis Heaven; yes,
        Heaven is the prize!

Yes, Heaven is the prize!
  My soul, oh! think of this:
All earthly goods despise
  For such a crown of bliss.
      'Tis Heaven, etc.

Yes, Heaven is the prize !
　　When sorrows press around,
Look up beyond the skies,
　　Where hope and strength are found.
　　　　'Tis Heaven, etc,

Yes, Heaven is the prize !
　　Oh ! 'tis not hard to gain.
He surely wins who tries ;
　　For hope can conquer pain.
　　　　'Tis Heaven, etc.

Yes, Heaven is the prize !
　　The strife will soon be past ;
Faint not, but raise your eyes,
　　And struggle to the last.
　　　　'Tis Heaven, etc,

Yes, Heaven is the prize !
　　Faith shows the crown to gain ;
Hope lights the way, and dies ;
　　But Love will always reign.
　　　　'Tis Heaven, etc.

Yes, Heaven is the prize !
　　Too much cannot be given ;

And he alone is wise
  Who gives up all for Heaven.
    'Tis Heaven, etc.

Yes, Heaven is the prize!
  Death opens wide the door,
And then the spirit flies
  To God for evermore.
    'Tis Heaven, etc.

THE COMMANDMENTS.

1. ONE God alone thou shalt adore,
   And daily love Him more and more.
2. Thou shalt not take His name in vain,
   Nor aught that's sacred e'er profane.
   Chorus.—Remember these Commandments,
       which were given
     To make us good on earth, and fit
       for heaven.

3. No servile work on Sunday do,
   And keep it ever holy, too.
4. Obedience to thy parents give,
   That thou mayest the longer live.
       Remember, etc.

5. Thy fellow-man thou shalt not kill,
   Nor even wish to do him ill.
6. Great purity thou shalt preserve,
   And from innocence never swerve.
      Remember, etc.

7. Thou shalt not steal nor, knowingly,
   Keep what belongeth not to thee.
8. Thou shalt not e'er false witness bear;
   To lie or slander never dare.
      Remember, etc.

9. Thy thoughts shall always modest be;
   Keep them from all uncleanness free.
10. With thy possessions be content;
    Thus wilt thou keep this commandment.
       Remember, etc.

COMMANDMENTS OF THE CHURCH.

1. ON Sundays, holydays likewise,
   Attend the Holy Sacrifice.
2. All fasts and days of abstinence
   Keep strictly in the Church's sense.

for Catholic Children.

Cho. Remember these Commandments, which were given
To make us good on earth, and fit for Heaven.

3. Remember, at least once a year,
Confess thy sins, thy conscience clear.
4. Receive Communion once a year,
At Easter-time, with holy fear.
Remember, etc.

5. The Church commands that tithes we pay;
Her commandment let us obey.
6. Solemnize not marriage in Lent;
The same precept keep in Advent.
Remember, etc.

THE SEVEN SACRAMENTS.

THE Church has seven Sacraments,
As we must all believe :
These means of grace we all must seek
To know or to receive.

1st, Baptism washes out the sin
Which Adam did commit.

2d, The sins which we ourselves have done
   True Penance will remit.
3d, The Holy Eucharist is the
   Body and Blood divine
Of Jesus Christ, both God and man,
   In form of bread and wine.
4th, In Confirmation, we believe,
   The Holy Ghost is given;
5th, In Extreme Unction we get grace,
   To die in hope of heaven.
6th, In Holy Orders, the Bishops
   And Priests get power and grace.
7th, And Matrimony blesses those
   Who married life embrace.

All praise and thanks to Jesus be,
   And to His Precious Blood,
By which we have the Sacraments,
   The source of every good!
                    Amen.

GREAT GOD, WE THANK THEE.

GREAT God, we thank Thee for the grace
   Of hearing Holy Mass this day.
On Sundays, may we always come
   To hear the Holy Mass, and pray.

Then may the grace of Holy Mass
   Be with us still in all our need,
And keep us from the stain of sin,
   In every thought, and word, and deed.
                         Amen.

HAPPY WE WHO, THUS UNITED.

HAPPY we who, thus united,
   Join in cheerful melody;
Praising Jesus, Mary, Joseph,
   In the " Holy Family."
     Jesus, Mary, Joseph, help us,
       That we ever true may be
     To the promises that bind us
       To the " Holy Family."

Hymns and Songs

Jesus, whose almighty bidding
  All created things fulfil,
Lives on earth in meek subjection
  To his earthly parents' will.
    Sweetest Infant, make us patient
    And obedient for Thy sake ;
    Teach us to be chaste and gentle,
    All our stormy passions break.

Mary ! thou alone wert chosen
  To be Mother of thy Lord :
Thou didst guide the early footsteps
  Of the Great Incarnate Word.
    Dearest Mother ! make us humble ;
    For thy Son will take His rest
    In the poor and lowly dwelling
    Of a humble sinner's breast.

Joseph ! thou wert called the father
  Of thy Maker and thy Lord ;
Thine it was to save thy Saviour
  From the cruel Herod's sword.
    Suffer us to call thee father ;
    Show to us a father's love ;
    Lead us safe through every danger
    Till we meet in heaven above.

GOD BLESS OUR POPE.

FULL in the panting heart of Rome,
   Beneath th' Apostles' crowning dome,
From pilgrims' lips that kiss the ground,
Breathes in all tongues one only sound—
   God bless our Pope, the great, the good!

The golden roof, the marble walls,
The Vatican's majestic halls,
The note redouble, till it fills
With echoes sweet the Seven Hills—
   God bless our Pope, the great, the good!

From torrid south to frozen north
The wave harmonious stretches forth,
Yet strikes no chord more true to Rome's
Than rings within our hearts and homes—
   God bless our Pope, the great, the good!

For, like the sparks of unseen fire
That speak along the magic wire,
From home to home, from heart to heart,
These words of countless children dart—
   God bless our Pope, the great, the good!

To homes and hearts of saints above,
Which linked with ours in thought and love,
Repeating, bless the pilgrims' strain,
As showers enrich with borrowed rain—
    God bless our Pope, the great, the good!

BLEST IS THE FAITH, DIVINE AND STRONG.

BLEST is the faith, divine and strong,
    Of thanks and praise an endless fountain,
Whose life is one perpetual song,
    High up the Saviour's holy mountain.
Cho. Oh! Sion's songs are sweet to sing,
    With melodies of gladness laden;
    Hark how the harps of angels ring!
    Hail, Son of Man! Hail, Mother-Maiden!

Blest is the hope that holds to God
    In doubt and darkness still unshaken,
And sings along the heavenly road
    Sweetest when most it seems forsaken.
    Oh! Sion's songs, etc.

Blest is the love that cannot love
  Aught that earth gives of best and brightest,
Whose raptures thrill like saints above
  Most when its earthly gifts are lightest.
    Oh! Sion's songs, etc.

FAITH OF OUR FATHERS.

FAITH of our fathers! living still,
  In spite of dungeon, fire, and sword;
Oh! how our hearts beat high with joy
  Whene'er we hear that glorious word.
    Faith of our fathers! Holy Faith!
    We will be true to thee till death.

Our fathers, chained in prisons dark,
  Were still in heart and conscience free;
How sweet would be their children's fate,
  If they, like them, could die for thee!
    Faith of our Fathers! etc.

Faith of our fathers! Mary's prayers
  Shall win our country soon to thee;
And through the truth that comes from God,
  Oh! then, indeed, we shall be free.
    Faith of our fathers! etc.

Faith of our fathers! we will love
   Both friend and foe in all our strife;
And preach thee, too, as love knows how,
   By kindly words and virtuous life.
     Faith of our fathers! etc.

F. W. Faber

THE CHURCH OF THE SAINTS.

'LL never forsake thee; I never will be,
   O Church of the Saints! an apostate from thee;
Though friends may entice me, and fortune may frown,
My Faith and my Church unto death I will own.

They may boast of their wealth, they may talk of their gold,
I'll be true to the faith like the martyrs of old.
"A Catholic live, and a Catholic die!"
Be this my life's watchword, at death my last cry.

I may lose some advantage and forfeit some gain,

I may meet with unkindness and suffer some
   pain ;
But Jesus and Mary will surely bestow
Richer gifts than from sin and apostasy flow.

Then we'll cling to the priest, and we'll cling
   to the Pope ;
We'll cling to Christ's Vicar, for Christ is our
   hope ;
We'll fight a good battle, and Mary the while
From her throne in the skies on her children
   will smile.

I AM A LITTLE CATHOLIC.

I AM a little Catholic,
   And Christian is my name,
And I believe the Holy Church
   In every age the same.

I love her altars where I kneel
   My Jesus to adore ;
I love my Mother, Mary dear ;
   Oh ! may I love them more.

I love the saints of olden time,
  The places where they dwelt;
I love to pray where saints have prayed,
  And kneel where they have knelt.

I love the Holy Sacraments,
  They bring me near to God;
The Church points out the way to heaven
  These help me on the road.

I love the priests, my pastors dear,
  They have left all for me;
Next to my parents here on earth,
  I love them tenderly.

I am a little Catholic,
  I love my Holy Faith;
I will be true to Holy Church,
  And steadfast until death.

TWO THOUSAND YEARS AGO.

TWO thousand years, two thousand years,
  Our bark o'er billowy seas
Has onward kept her steady course,
  Through hurricane and breeze.

Her Captain was the Risen One—
  She braved the stormy foe:
And still He guides who guided her
  Two thousand years ago!
    And still He guides, etc.

When first our gallant ship was launched,
  Although our hands were few,
Yet dauntless was each bosom found,
  And every heart was true;
And still though in her mighty hull
  Unnumbered bosoms glow,
Her crew is faithful as it was
  Two thousand years ago!

True, some had left this noble craft,
  To sail the seas alone,
And made them, in their hour of pride,
  A vessel of their own;
But, when portentous clouds did rise,
  Tempestuous storms did blow,
They re-entered that old vessel built
  Two thousand years ago!

For onward rides our gallant bark,
  With all her canvas set,

In some few nations still unknown
  To plant her standards yet :
Her flag shall float where'er a breath
  From human life shall glow,
And millions bless the bark that sailed
  Two thousand years ago.

True to that guiding star which led
  To Israel's cradled hope,
Her steady needle pointeth yet
  To Calvary's bloody top!
Yes! there she floats, that good old ship,
  From mast to keel below
Sea-worthy still, as erst she was
  Two thousand years ago.

Not unto us—not unto us—
  Be praise or glory given,
But unto Him who watch and ward
  Hath kept for her in heaven,
Who quelled the whirlwind in its wrath,
  Bade tempests cease to blow!—
The Lord, who launched our vessel forth
  Two thousand years ago.

Then onward speed thee, brave old bark,
  Speed onward in thy pride,

O'er sunny seas and billows dark,
  The Holy One thy guide;
And sacred be each plank and spar,
  Unchanged by friend or foe,
Just as she left Jerusalem
  Two thousand years ago!

THE SIGN OF THE CROSS.

A CHILD of God! remember,
  When thou to Christ wast born,
How then across thine infant breast
  His sacred Sign was drawn.

And when confirming Chrism
  Upon thy brow was laid,
How in that sign the Holy Ghost
  His grace upon thee shed.

Therefore, when sleep invites thee
  To take thy needful rest,
Be sure that with the Sacred Cross
  Thou sign thy brow and breast.

The Cross hath wondrous virtue
  All evil to control;
To scatter darkness and to calm
  The tempest of the soul.

What though in sleep this body
  May helpless seem to lie?
I nothing fear, assured that One
  Stronger than all is nigh.

On Him my heart shall ponder
  E'en while my rest I take,
My shield and shelter while I sleep,
  My joy when I awake.

CHRISTIANS, TO THE WAR!

CHRISTIANS, to the war! gather from afar!
  Hark, hark! the word is given:
Jesus bids us fight "for God and the right,"
  And for Mary, the Queen of Heaven.
Now first for thee, thou wicked world,
  Puffed up with godless pomp and pageant,
Avenging grace to humble thee
  Can make the weakest arm its agent.
    Christians, to the war! etc.

And thou, dark fiend, six thousand years
   The Bride of Christ in vain tormenting,
Shall find our hate and scorn of thee
   Deep as thine own and unrelenting.
           Christians, to the war! etc.

Ah self! so oft forgiven, thou
   Canst play no part but that of traitor;
We spare thy life, but thou must bear
   The felon's brand, the captive's fetter.
           Christians, to the war! etc.

But worse than devil, flesh, or world,
   Human respect, like poison creeping,
Chills and unnerves the hosts of Christ,
   When weary, war-worn hearts are sleeping.
           Christians, to the war! etc.

Like lions roaring for their prey,
   Armies of foes are round us trooping;
What then? See! countless angels come
   To heal the hurt, to raise the drooping.
           Christians, to the war! etc.

Then bravely, comrades, to the fight,
   With shout and song each other cheering;

Strength not our own from heaven descends—
  The sun breaks out, the clouds are clearing.
    Christians, to the war! etc.

On to the gates of Sion, on!
  Break through the foe with fresh endeavor;
We'll hang our colors up in heaven,
  When peace shall be proclaimed for ever.
    Christians, to the war! etc.

— *F W Faber*

OFT IN DANGER, OFT IN WOE.

OFT in danger, oft in woe,
  Onward, Christians, onward go!
Bear the toil, maintain the strife,
  Strengthened with the Bread of Life.

Let not sorrow dim your eye,
  Soon shall every tear be dry;
Let not fear your course impede,
  Great your strength if great your need.

Let your drooping hearts be glad;
  March in heavenly armor clad;
Fight, nor think the battle long,
  Soon shall vict'ry wake your song.

Firm in faith, and strong by love
  More than conquerors ye shall prove;
Though opposed by many a foe,
  Christian soldiers, onward go!

Lord of might and majesty,
  Grant to us the victory;
Holy Father, Holy Son,
  Holy Spirit, Three in One!

SUMMER'S DEPARTURE.

THE glory of Summer
  Is faded and fled;
The wreaths that adorned her
  Are dying and dead;
The Autumn is coming,
  And, strong in his blast,
Will open to Winter
  A passage at last.

Oh! how to my spirit
  It seemeth to say:
"Thus, too, is thy Summer
  Fast fleeting away;

And the things which thou lovest,
　　Though pleasant they be,
And the friends thou hast chosen,
　　Are fading with thee.

" Dost thou covet a Summer
　　More certain of bliss?
Go seek thee a country
　　Far brighter than this;
Where the joys thou hast lost
　　Thou shalt never deplore,
And the friends thou hast chosen
　　Shall quit thee no more."

DECAY.

THE leaves around me falling
　　Are preaching of decay:
The hollow winds are calling,
　　" Come, pilgrim, haste away!"
The day in night declining
　　Says, I must, too, decline;
The year, its life resigning,
　　Its lot foreshadows mine.

The lights my path surrounding,
　The helps to which I cling,
The hopes within me bounding,
　The joys that round me wing,
All, all, like stars at even,
　Just gleam to shoot away;
Pass on before to heaven,
　And chide at my delay.

The friends gone there before me
　Are calling from on high;
And joyous angels o'er me
　Are beckoning from the sky.
" Why wait," they sing, " and wither
　'Mid scenes of death and sin?
'Tis better to come hither,
　And find true life begin."

I hear the invitation,
　And fain would rise and come,
A sinner to salvation,
　An exile to his home.
But, while I here must linger,
　Thus, thus let all I see
Point out with faithful finger
　To heaven, O Lord! and Thee.

PLAINT FOR THE DEAD.

WHEN thou hast conquered! then at last
   Thy course is run—good-night!
Thou art well pleased that it is past,
   Beyond the grave 'tis light.
But ye, dear friends whom she must leave,
   Look up, and say, Farewell!
Why should ye thus lament and grieve?
   With her it standeth well.

Henceforth a life of joy she shares
   In her Creator's hand;
None of the griefs can touch her there
   That haunt this lower land.
Far better is a happy death
   Than worldly life, I trow;
The weakness once she sank beneath
   She nevermore shall know.

Lay on her coffin many a wreath,
   For conquerors wreathed are seen;
And lo! her soul attains through death
   The crown of evergreen.
That we should see her grave, alas!
   Shows we are frail, indeed;

That it so soon should come to pass,
  Our Father hath decreed.

'Twas but a while that she was sent
  To dwell among us here;
Now God resumes what He has lent,
  Oh! grieve not o'er her bier;
But say, 'twas given at His command—
  Who takes it; He is just;
Our life and death are in His hand,
  His servants can but trust.

Tho' dead, she speaks, "Dear friends, be still,
  Think not too young am I;
For she who dies as God doth will
  Is old enough to die."
Father! it is a bitter pang
  For frail, weak hearts to bear;
Forgive us if we can't return
  Thy loan without a tear.

This thought alone our souls shall cheer:
  To us the boon was given,
Here in a sinful world to rear
  One angel soul for heaven.

Ah! when shall that great day be come,
  When these things fade away,
And Thou shalt bid us welcome home?
  Would God it were to-day!

EVENING.
THE NIGHT IS COME.

THE night is come, wherein at last we res
  God order this and all things for th best;
Beneath His blessing fearless may we lie,
  Since He is nigh.

Drive evil thoughts and spirits far away;
O Father! watch o'er us till dawning day;
Body and soul alike from harm defend—
  Thine angels send.

Let holy prayers and thoughts our latest be;
Let us awake with joy still close to Thee;
In all serve Thee, in every deed and thought
  Thy praise be sought.

Give to the sick, as Thy beloved, sleep;
And help the captive, comfort those who weep;
Care for the widows' and the orphans' woe;
    Keep far our foe.

Father, Thy Name be praised, Thy Kingdom
    come,
Thy will be wrought as in our heavenly home;
Keep us in life, forgive our sins, deliver
    Us now and ever. Amen.

THE COMMENDATION.

NOW with the fast-departing light,
    Maker of all, we ask of Thee,
Of Thy great goodness, through the night
    Our guardian and defence to be.

Far off let idle visions fly,
    No phantom of the night molest;
Curb Thou our raging enemy,
    That we in chaste repose may rest.

Father of Mercies! hear our cry,
    Hear us, thou Sole-begotten Son,
Who, with the Holy Ghost most high,
    Reignest while endless ages run.
                      Amen.

HEAR THY CHILDREN, GENTLE JESUS.

EAR Thy children, gentle Jesus,
   While we breathe our evening prayer;
Save us from all harm and danger,
   Take us 'neath Thy shelt'ring care.

Save us from the wiles of Satan,
   'Mid the lone and sleepful night;
Sweetly may bright guardian angels
   Keep us 'neath their watchful sight.

Gentle Jesus, look in pity
   From Thy great white throne above·
All the night Thy heart is wakeful
   In Thy sacrament of love.

Shades of even fast are falling,
   Day is fading into gloom;
When the shades of death fall round us,
   Lead Thine exiled children home.

OUR EVENING HYMN.

SWEET Saviour, bless us ere we go;
   Thy word into our minds instill;
And make our lukewarm hearts to glow
   With lowly love and fervent will.
      Through life's long day and death's
         dark night,
     O gentle Jesus! be our light.

The day is done, its hours have run,
   And Thou hast taken count of all—
The scanty triumphs grace hath won,
   The broken vow, the frequent fall.
     Through life's long day, etc.

Grant us, dear Lord, from evil ways
   True absolution and release,
And bless us more than in past days
   With purity and inward peace.
     Through life's long day, etc.

Do more than pardon: give us joy,
   Sweet fear, and sober liberty;
And simple hearts without alloy,
   That only long to be like Thee.
     Through life's long day, etc.

Labor is sweet, for Thou hast toiled ;
  And care is light, for thou hast cared ;
Ah ! never let our works be soiled
  With strife, or by deceit ensnared.
    Through life's long day, etc.

For all we love, the poor, the sad,
  The sinful—unto Thee we call.
Oh ! let Thy mercy make us glad—
  Thou art our Jesus and our All.
    Through life's long day, etc.

Sweet Saviour, bless us, night is come ;
  Mary and Joseph, near us be ;
Good Angels, watch about our home;
  And we are one day nearer Thee.
    Through life's long day, etc.

MISSIONS.

THE SINNER INVITED TO THE MISSION.

H ! come to thy merciful Saviour who calls you,
Oh ! come to thy Lord, who forgives and forgets:

Though dark be the fortune on earth that befalls you,
  There's a bright home above where the sun never sets.
Oh! come, then, to Jesus, whose arms are extended
  To fold His dear children in closest embrace!
Oh! come, for your exile will shortly be ended,
  And Jesus will show you His beautiful face.

Then come to the Saviour, whose mercy grows brighter
  The longer you look at the depth of His love;
And fear not, 'tis Jesus, and life's cares grow lighter
  As you think of the home and the glory above.
Oh! come, then, to Jesus, and say how you love Him,
  And swear at his feet you will keep in His grace;
For one tear that is shed by a sinner can move Him,
  And your sins will drop off in His tender embrace.

Then come to His feet, and lay open your story
Of suffering and sorrow, of guilt and of shame;
For the pardon of sin is the crown of His glory,
And the joy of our Lord to be true to His name.

Amen.

HAIL, HOLY MISSION!

HAIL, holy Mission, hail!
   Sighing, we turn to thee,
For weary have we found
   The path of sin to be.

Hail, holy Mission, hail!
   Sent to us from above,
When Jesus with His cross
   Comes to win back our love.

Hail, holy Mission, hail!
   Time of repentant tears,
When to the soul returns
   The peace of former years.

Hail, holy Mission, hail !
    Sweet time of humble prayer,
When rests the soul on God,
    Freed from this dark world's care.

Hail, holy Mission, hail !
    Time of all others blessed,
When in the loving soul
    Jesus takes up His rest.

Hail, holy Mission, hail !
    Foretaste of joys above,
O Jesus ! make our hearts
    Burn with Thy tender love.

FOR PROCESSIONS.

BRIGHTLY GLEAMS OUR BANNER.

BRIGHTLY gleams our banner,
    Pointing to the sky,
Waving wand'rers onwards,
    To their home on high.

Hail, O holy banner!
  Gladly thus we pray,
And with hearts united
  Take our heavenward way.
        Brightly gleams, etc.

Hail, sweet Jesus! Master!
  Round Thy sacred feet,
Now, with hearts rejoicing,
  See Thy children meet.
Long, alas, we've left Thee,
  Straying far away;
But once more we enter
  On the "narrow way."
        Brightly gleams, etc.

Mary! Mother! Ave!
  Israel's Lily, hail!
Comfort of thy children
  In this sinful vale.
'Mid life's surging ocean,
  Whither shall we flee,
Save, O stainless Virgin!
  Mother, unto thee?
        Brightly gleams, etc.

Ave! Joseph! Ave!
  Chaste and spotless flower;
Cast thy mantle o'er us
  At death's solemn hour.
Be our father, ever,
  Joseph, meek and mild,
Chaste spouse of our Mother,
  Keeper of her Child.
        Brightly gleams, etc.

Jesus! Mary! Joseph!
  Sweet and holy Three,
List the praise we pay you
  On our bended knee.
May we sing your glory
  In glad realms above,
Bound for ever to you
  By the bonds of love.
      Brightly gleams our banner,
        Pointing to the sky,
      Waving wand'rers onwards,
        To their home on high.
              Amen.

ONWARD! CHRISTIAN SOLDIERS.

NWARD! Christian soldiers,
  Marching, as to war,
With the cross of Jesus
  Going on before.
Christ, the Royal Master,
  Leads against the foe.
Forward into battle,
  See, his banners go.
    Onward! Christian soldiers, etc.

At the sign of triumph
  Satan's host doth flee;
On, then, Christian soldiers,
  On to victory.
Hell's foundations quiver
  At the shout of praise;
Brothers, lift your voices,
  Loud your anthems raise.
    Onward! Christian soldiers, etc.

Like a mighty army,
  Moves the Church of God:
Brothers, we are treading
  Where the saints have trod;

We are not divided,
  All one body we,
One in hope and doctrine,
  One in charity.
    Onward ! Christian soldiers, etc.

Crowns and thrones may perish,
  Kingdoms rise and wane,
But the Church of Jesus
  Constant will remain.
Gates of hell can never
  'Gainst that Church prevail ;
We have Christ's own promise,
  And that cannot fail.
    Onward ! Christian soldiers, etc.

Onward, then, ye people,
  Join our happy throng,
Blend with ours your voices,
  In the triumph song :
Glory, laud, and honor,
  Unto Christ the King—
This, through endless ages,
  Men and angels sing.
    Onward ! Christian soldiers, etc.

Baring Gould

OUR NATIVE LAND.

WHAT is that land of sweetest name,
  Dearest to us of all the world?
What is that soil which freemen claim?
  Whose is the flag no foe hath furled?
Chorus.—'Tis the land of the free and the home
    of the brave:
  Long may her starry banner wave!
  United for ever in heart and in hand,
  God keep and save our native land!

What is that land the exile loves,
  When through the world he's forced to roam?
Where do they fly like weary doves,
  Seeking a free and happy home?
            Chorus.

What is that land where faith is free,
  Where we can worship God in peace?
Where is this sweetest liberty?
  Oh! may this freedom never cease.
            Chorus.

Praise we the land that gave us birth !
Dear is the land we call our own !
Well may we sing in gleeful mirth ;
Well may we love but her alone !
                              Chorus.

THE LORD'S PRAYER.

OUR *Father who art in heaven—*
   Mighty one, all else above—
Throned 'mid angels and archangels,
   Yet dost bend to human love ;
*Hallowed be Thy name, Thy kingdom
   Come* to every heathen land ;
Where the sinner walks in darkness,
   Stretch to him Thy guiding hand.

Yet we ask not for a pathway
   Where no martyr crown is won,
Rather give us faith to suffer,
   And still say *Thy will be done.*
Faith to love what Thou hast given,
   Whatsoe'er Thy mandate be,
Till *on earth as 'tis in heaven*,
   Every spirit bows to Thee.

Neither seek we fame and splendor,
 Save us from the snares they spread,
But, as best befits us, Father—
Give this day our daily bread;
All our needs Thy wisdom knoweth,
 How unworthy—well we know,
And what good Thy hand bestoweth—
 We to Thy vast mercy owe.

Oh! how oft our steps have wandered
 In the ways Thou badest us shun—
Oh! what deeds of gilt have grieved Thee!
 Oh! what duties left undone!
Pardon Thou each erring brother;
 Help us to return and live,
And as we forgive each other,
So our trespasses forgive.

Lead us not into temptation
 When the enemy is strong,
For too prone each inclination
 Ever is to turn to wrong;
Grace of Thine is all sufficient
 Leave us not to fall again,
But deliver us from evil
 Now and evermore. *Amen.*

BENEDICTION TO THE MOST HOLY SACRAMENT.

O SALUTARIS HOSTIA.

 SALUTARIS Hostia,
   Quæ cœli pandis ostium:
Bella premunt hostilia,
   Da robur, fer auxilium.

Uni Trinoque Domino
   Sit sempiterna gloria,
Qui vitam sine termino
   Nobis donet in patria.

TANTUM ERGO.

Tantum ergo Sacramentum,	Down in adoration falling.
Veneremur cernui;	Lo! the Sacred Host we hail:
Et antiquum documentum,	Lo! o'er ancient forms departing
Novo cedat ritui:	Newer rites of grace
Præstet fides supplementum	prevail:
Sensuum defectui.	Faith for all defects supplying,
	Where the feeble senses fail.

Genitori, Genitoque,
 Laus et jubilatio,
Salus, honor, virtus quoque,
 Sit et benedictio:
Procedenti ab utroque,
 Compar sit laudatio.
  Amen.

To the Everlasting Father
 And the Son who reigns
  on high,
With the Holy Ghost proceeding
 Forth from both eternally,
Be salvation, honor, blessing,
 Equal might and majesty.
  Amen.

V. Panem de cœlo præstitisti eis.
R. Omne delectamentum in se habentem.

V. Thou hast given them bread from heaven.
R. Full of all sweetness and delight.

OREMUS:

Deus, qui nobis sub Sacramento mirabili, Passionis tuæ memoriam reliquisti: tribue, quæsumus, ita nos corporis et sanguinis tui sacra mysteria venerari, ut redemptionis tuæ fructum in no-

LET US PRAY:

O God, who has left us in this wonderful Sacrament a perpetual memorial of Thy Passion: Grant us, we beseech Thee, so to reverence the sacred mysteries of Thy body and blood, that we

bis jugiter sentiamus. Qui vivis et regnas in sæcula sæculorum. Amen. may continually find in our souls the fruit of Thy redemption; Thou who livest and reignest world without end. Amen.

ADORO TE.

Adoro Te devote, latens Deitas,
Quæ sub his figuris vere latitas:
Tibi se cor meum totum subjicit,
Quia Te contemplans, totum deficit.

Chorus.
Ave Jesu, Pastor fidelium,
Adauge fidem omnium in te credentium.

O COR JESU.

O cor Jesu, amoris victima, sis mihi salus in mpore tribulationis, et in hora mortis; et dic animæ meæ: Salus tua ego sum, Alleluia.

AVE VERUM.

Ave verum corpus natum de Maria Virgine,
Vere passum, immolatum in Cruce pro homine.
Cujus latus perforatum unda fluxit et sanguine.
Esto nobis præguslatum mortis in examine.
O dulcis! O pie! O Jesu, Fili Mariæ!
Amen.

THE SODALITY OFFICE.

The reader begins :
V. Let us pray for a blessing.

The Blessing.
May the Lord Almighty grant us a quiet night and a perfect end.
R. Amen.

The Lesson.—St. John, Epistle III.
Dearly beloved, if our heart do not reproach us, we have confidence in God. And whatsoever we shall ask we shall receive of Him; because we keep His commandments, and do those things which are pleasing in His sight. And this is His commandment: that we should believe in the name of His Son Jesus Christ, and love one another, as He has given commandment unto us. And do Thou, O Lord, have mercy upon us.
R. Thanks be to God.
V. Our help is in the name of the Lord.
R. Who hath made heaven and earth.
Our Father, etc. (*All in secret.*)
Then the Rev. Director makes the confession :
I confess to Almighty God, etc.

All answer. May the Almighty God have mercy on thee, forgive thee thy sins, and bring thee to life everlasting.

R. Amen.

All repeat the confession :

I confess to Almighty God, to Blessed Mary ever Virgin, to Blessed Michael the Archangel, to Blessed John the Baptist, to the Holy Apostles Peter and Paul, to all the Saints, and to you, father, that I have sinned exceedingly in thought, word, and deed, through my fault, through my fault, through my most grievous fault. Therefore I beseech the Blessed Mary ever Virgin, Blessed Michael the Archangel, Blessed John the Baptist, the Holy Apostles Peter and Paul, all the Saints, and you, father, to pray to the Lord our God for me.

The Rev. Director says :

May the Almighty God have mercy upon you, forgive you your sins, and bring you to life everlasting.

R. Amen.

May the Almighty and Merciful Lord grant us pardon, absolution, and remission of our sins.

R. Amen.

V. Convert us, O God our Saviour.

R. And turn away Thine anger from us.

V. O God, stretch forth to aid me.

R. O Lord, make haste to help me.

Glory be to the Father, etc.

As it was in the beginning, etc.
Ant. Have mercy on me, O Lord.

In Paschal Time.

Ant. Alleluia.

PSALM IV.

When I called upon Him, the God of my justice, heard me :* when I was in distress, Thou didst enlarge me.

Have mercy upon me :* and hear my prayer.

O ye sons of men, how long will ye be dull of heart :* why do ye love vanity and seek after lying ?

Know ye also that the Lord hath exalted His Holy One :* the Lord will hear me when I cry unto Him.

Be ye angry and sin not :* the things ye say in your hearts be sorry for upon your beds.

Offer the sacrifice of justice, and trust in the Lord :* many say, Who showeth us good things ?

The light of Thy countenance, O Lord, is signed upon us :* Thou hast given gladness to my heart.

By the fruit of their corn, their wine, and oil :* are they multiplied.

In peace in the self-same :* I will sleep, and I will rest.

For Thou, O Lord, alone :* hast established me in hope.

Glory be to the Father, etc.

PSALM XXX.

In Thee, O Lord, have I hoped ; let me never be confounded :* Deliver me in thy justice.

Bow down Thine ear unto me :* make haste to deliver me.

Be Thou unto me a God, a protector, and a house of refuge :* that Thou mayest save me.

For Thou art my strength and my refuge :* and for Thy name's sake Thou wilt lead me and nourish me.

Thou wilt bring me out of this snare which they have hid from me :* for Thou art my protector.

Into Thy hands I commend my spirit :* Thou hast redeemed me, O Lord the God of truth.

Glory be to the Father, etc.

PSALM XC.

He that dwelleth in the aid of the Most High :* shall abide under the protection of the God of Heaven.

He shall say unto the Lord, Thou art my protector and my refuge :* My God, in Him will I trust.

For He hath delivered me from the snare of the hunters :* and from the sharp word.

He shall overshadow thee with His shoulders :* and under His wings thou shalt trust.

His truth shall compass thee with a shield :* thou shall not be afraid of the terror of the night,

Nor of the arrow that flieth in the day, or the plague

that walketh about in the dark :* or of the assault of the evil one in the noon-day.

A thousand shall fall at thy side, and ten thousand at thy right hand :* but it shall not come nigh unto thee.

But thou shalt consider with thine eyes :* and shalt see the reward of the wicked.

Because Thou, O Lord, art my hope :* Thou hast made the Most High Thy refuge.

There shall no evil approach unto thee :* neither shall the scourge come near thy dwelling.

For He hath given His angels charge over thee :* to keep thee in all thy ways.

In their hands they shall bear thee up :* lest thou dash thy foot against a stone.

Thou shalt walk upon the asp and the basilisk :* and thou shalt trample under foot the lion and the dragon.

Because he hath hoped in me I will deliver him :* I will protect him, because he hath known my name.

He shall cry to me, and I will hear him :* I am with him in tribulation : I will deliver him, and I will glorify him.

I will fill him with length of days :* and I will show him my salvation.

Glory be to the Father, etc.

PSALM CXXXIII.

Behold now, bless ye the Lord :* all ye servants of the Lord :
Who stand in the house of the Lord :* in the courts of the house of our God.
Lift up your hands by night to the holy places :* and bless ye the Lord.
May the Lord out of Sion bless thee :* He that hath made heaven and earth.
Glory be to the Father, etc.
Ant. Have mercy on me, O Lord, and hear my prayer.

In Paschal Time.
Ant. Alleluia, Alleluia, Alleluia.

HYMN.

Before the daylight sinks away,
Creator! God, whom all obey,
In mercy guard our souls from ill,
Be thou our kind protector still.

May dreams delusive far recede,
Nor phantoms our repose impede ;
Let no dark fiend to crime allure,
From all defilement keep us pure.

Thy grace, O Father! may we share,
Co-equal Son! receive our prayer;
Enthroned, O Holy Ghost! with Thee,
Eternal Godhead! One in Three. Amen.

Little Chapter.—*Jerem.* xiv.

But Thou, O Lord, art among us, and Thy holy name is invoked upon us; forsake us not, O Lord our God.

R. Thanks be to God.

Short Resp. Into Thy hands, O Lord, I commend my spirit. Into Thy hands, etc.

V. For Thou has redeemed us, O Lord, the God of truth.

I commend, etc.

Glory be to the Father, etc.

Into Thy hands, etc.

V. Keep us, O Lord, as the apple of thine eye.

R. Protect us under the shadow of thy wings.

In Paschal Time the above is said thus:

Short Resp. Into thy hands, O Lord, I commend my spirit. Alleluia, Alleluia. Into thy hands, etc.

V. For Thou hast redeemed us, O Lord, the God of truth. Alleluia, Alleluia.

Glory be to the Father, etc.

Into Thy hands, etc.

V. Keep us, O Lord, as the apple of thine eye. Alleluia.
R. Protect us under the shadow of Thy wings. Alleluia.
Ant. Save us, O Lord.

CANTICLE OF SIMEON.—St. Luke ii.

Now, O Lord, Thou dost dismiss Thy servant,* according to Thy word, in peace ;
Because mine eyes* have seen Thy salvation :
Which Thou hast prepared,* before the face of all peoples :
A light to the revelation of the Gentiles,* and the glory of thy people Israel.
Glory be to the Father, etc.
Ant. Save us, O Lord, while we are awake ; keep us while we sleep, that we may watch with Christ and rest in peace.

(*In Paschal Time*, Alleluia.)

The following prayers are omitted on Doubles and within Octaves :
Lord, have mercy on us.
Christ, have mercy on us.
Lord, have mercy on us.
Our Father, etc. (*In secret.*)
V. And lead us not into temptation.
R. But deliver us from evil.

I believe in God, etc. (*In secret.*)
V. The resurrection of the body,
R. And life everlasting. Amen.
V. Blessed art thou, O Lord God of our fathers.
R. Worthy to be praised and glorious for ever.
V. Let us bless the Father and the Son, with the Holy Ghost.
R. Let us praise and exalt him for ever.
V. Blessed art Thou, O Lord, in the firmament of heaven.
R. Worthy to be praised and glorious and exalted for ever.
V. May the Almighty and Merciful Lord bless and preserve us.
R. Amen.
V. Vouchsafe, O Lord, this night
R. To keep us without sin.
V. Have mercy on us, O Lord.
R. Have mercy on us.
V. Let thy mercy, O Lord, be upon us.
R. As we have hoped in Thee,
V. O Lord, hear my prayer,
R. And let my cry come unto Thee.
V. The Lord be with you,
R. And with thy Spirit.

Let us pray.

Visit, we beseech Thee, O Lord, this habitation, and

drive far from it all snares of the enemy. Let Thy holy angels dwell therein, who may keep us in peace ; and may Thy blessing be always upon us. Through Jesus Christ, Thy Son, Our Lord, etc.
V. The Lord be with you
R. And with thy Spirit.
V. Let us bless the Lord.
R. Thanks be to God.

The Blessing.

May the Almighty and Merciful Lord, Father, Son, and Holy Ghost, bless and preserve us.
R. Amen.

MAJESTY DINVINE !

Full of glory, full of wonders,
   Majesty Divine !
'Mid Thine everlasting thunders
   How Thy lightnings shine !
Shoreless Ocean, who shall sound Thee ?
Thine eternity is round Thee,
   Majesty Divine !

Thou art grandly, always only,
   God in unity ;
Timeless, spaceless, single, lonely,
   Yet sublimely Three ;

Lone in grandeur, lone in glory,
Who shall tell Thy wond'rous story,
   Awful Trinity?

Speechlessly, without beginning,
   Sun that never rose;
Vast, adorable, and winning,
   Day that hath no close;
Bliss from Thine own glory tasting,
Everliving, everlasting,
   Life that never grows.

Glories over glories streaming
   All translucent shine;
Splendor still o'er splendors beaming,
   Change and intertwine;
Praises, blessings, adorations,
Greet Thee from the trembling nations,
   Majesty Divine!

O COME, O COME, EMMANUEL.

O come, O come, Emmanuel,
And ransom captive Israel,
That mourns in lonely exile here
Until the Son of God appear.
      Rejoice! rejoice! Emmanuel
      Shall come to thee, O Israel!

for Catholic Children.

O come, Thou Rod of Jesse, free
Thine own from Satan's tyranny;
From depths of hell Thy people save,
And give them victory o'er the grave.
    Rejoice! rejoice! etc.

O come, Thou Day-Spring, come and cheer
Our spirits by Thine advent here;
Disperse the gloomy clouds of night,
And death's dark shadows put to flight.
    Rejoice! rejoice! etc.

O come, Thou Key of David, come
And open wide our heavenly home;
Make safe the way that leads on high,
And close the path to misery.
    Rejoice! rejoice! etc.

O come, O come, Thou Lord of Might
Who to Thy tribes, on Sinai's height,
In ancient times didst give the law
In cloud, and majesty, and awe.
    Rejoice! rejoice! etc.

HOLY SPIRIT! LORD OF LIGHT!

Holy Spirit! Lord of light!
From Thy clear, celestial height
Thy pure, beaming radiance give.

Come, Thou Father of the poor!
Come with treasures which endure!
Come, Thou light of all that live.

Light immortal! Light divine!
Visit Thou these hearts of Thine,
And our inmost being fill.

If Thou take Thy grace away,
Nothing pure in man will stay:
All his good is turned to ill.

Heal our wounds, our strength renew;
On our dryness pour Thy dew;
Wash the stains of guilt away.

Bend the stubborn heart and will;
Melt the frozen, warm the chill;
Guide the steps that go astray.

Thou on those who evermore
Thee confess and Thee adore,
In Thy sevenfold gifts descend.

Give them comfort when they die,
Give them life with Thee on high,
Give them joys which never end.

Carswall F.

O WOUNDED HEART!

O wounded Heart! whence sprang
   The Church, the Saviour's Bride;
Thou Door of our Salvation's Ark
   Set in its mystic side—

Thou holy Fount! whence flows
   The sacred, sevenfold flood,
Where we our filthy robes may cleanse
   In the Lamb's saving blood—

By sorrowful relapse
   Thee will we rend no more;
But like Thy flames, those types of love,
   Strive Heavenward to soar.

O Jesu! Victim blest!
   What else but love divine
Could Thee constrain to open thus
   That sacred Heart of Thine?

O Fount of endless life!
   O Spring of waters clear!
O Flame celestial, cleansing all
   Who unto Thee draw near,

Hide me in Thy dear Heart,
  For thither do I fly ;
'There seek Thy grace through life, in death
  Thine immortality.

CLOSE VEILED IN THAT SWEET SACRAMENT.

Close veiled in that sweet sacrament,
  Our Jesus' heart, our treasure, lies ;
Love's priceless, dearest testament
  Is shrouded in that mystic guise.
Our Jesus left His realms of light,
  On wings of love to earth He's flown ;
To dwell with us 'tis his delight—
  He makes our hearts his dearest throne.

Chorus.

O Sacred Heart ! how sweet 'twould be
  If we could die for love of Thee.
O Sacred Heart ! how sweet 'twould be
  If we could die for love of Thee.

Love is not loved ! O angels ! weep ;
  Ye virgins chaste, breathe bitter sighs ;
O earth ! be clothed in mourning deep ;
  Withdraw your light, ye radiant skies :

For all our soul's dear Spouse hath died,
    For all His Heart with love doth burn;
Yet this meek Saviour men deride,
    And for His love make no return.
        Chorus.—O Sacred Heart ! etc.

That Heart for us could do no more,
    In anguish deep it sighed and bled;
A cruel spear pierced through its core,
    For us His last life's blood was shed.
That spear, O Jesus! pierced Thy Heart,
    That we within its depths might flee.
Oh ! wound our own with love's sweet dart—
    Let us expire for love of Thee.
        Chorus.—O Sacred Heart ! etc.

JESUS, I MY CROSS HAVE TAKEN.

Jesus, I my cross have taken,
    All to leave and follow Thee ;
I am poor, despised, forsaken—
    Thou henceforth my all shalt be.
Perish every fond ambition,
    All I've sought, or hoped, or known ;
Yet how rich is my condition—
    God and heaven may be mine own ?

Let the world despise and leave me :
  It has left my Saviour too ;
Human hearts and looks deceive me—
  Thou art not, like them, untrue.
Whilst Thy graces shall adorn me—
  God of wisdom, love, and might—
Foes may hate, and friends may scorn me;
  Show thy face, and all is bright.

Soul, then, know thy full salvation,
  Rise o'er sin, and fear, and care ;
Joy to find in every station
  Something still to do or bear.
Think what Spirit dwells within thee,
  Think what sacraments are thine '
Think that Jesus died to win thee—
  Child of heaven, canst thou repine ?

Haste thee on from grace to glory,
  Arm'd with faith, and winged with prayer
An eternal day before thee
  Waits for God to guide thee there.
Soon shall close thine earthly mission,
  Patience shall thy spirit raise ;
Hope shall change to glad fruition,
  Faith to sight, and prayer to praise.

Lyte

O VISION BRIGHT!

O vision bright! The glorious land of light
  Beams goldenly beyond the cloudless sky ;
'Mid heavenly fires, above all angel choirs,
  Sweet Mary, our dear Mother, reigns on high.

Chorus.

O vision bright! Angels' delight, Mary sits enthroned
  with Jesus nigh ;
When brighter far than either moon or star,
  Sweet Mary, our dear Mother, reigns on high.

O vision bright! In gentle, loving flight
  The Dove around his cherished Spouse doth fly ;
Where in that height of mercy's gentle might,
  Sweet Mary, our dear Mother, reigns on high.
    Chorus.—O vision bright! etc.

O vision bright! Th' eternal, dazzling light
  Of Jesus, her dear Son, we may descry ;
Her form He bears, her own sweet look he wears :
  Sweet Mary, our dear Mother, reigns on high.
    Chorus.—O vision bright! etc.

F. W. Faber.

HYMN FOR APOSTLES.

Now let the earth with joy resound,
And highest heav'n re-echo round ;
Nor heav'n nor earth too high can raise
The great Apostles' glorious praise.

O ye who, thron'd in glory dread,
Shall judge the living and the dead !
Lights of the world for evermore !
To you the suppliant prayer we pour.

Ye close the sacred gates on high ;
At your command apart they fly ;
Oh! loose us from the guilty chain
We strive to break, and strive in vain.

Sickness and health your voice obey;
At your command they go or stay;
Oh ! then from sin our souls restore ;
Increase our virtues more and more.

HYMN FOR A MARTYR.

O Thou ! of all thy warriors Lord,
Thyself the crown and sure reward,
Set us from sinful fetters free,
Who sing thy martyr's victory.

In selfish pleasures' worldly round
The taste of bitter gall he found;
But sweet to him was thy blest Name,
And thus to heavenly joys he came.

Right manfully his cross he bore,
And ran his race of torments sore:
For Thee he pour'd his life away;
With Thee he lives in endless day.

We, then, before Thee bending low,
Entreat Thee, Lord, thy love to show,
On this the day thy martyr died,
Who in thy saints are glorified.

HYMN FOR A BISHOP OR CONFESSOR.

Jesu! Thy priests' eternal prize!
   This day on us look down—
This day, that saw Thee in the skies
   Thy great Confessor crown.

Chosen for his fidelity,
   His love, and prudence rare;
The sheep Thy Father gave to Thee,
   Thou gavest to His care.

He knew and lov'd them, each and all;
  Their lambs he gently led;
They, too, in turn obeyed his call,
  And in his footsteps fed.

He met the wolf's impetuous shock,
  His cunning wiles defied;
And for his flock—his own dear flock—
  Was ready to have died.

Caswall tr 1858

HYMN FOR VIRGINS.

Thou crown of all the virgin choir!
  That holy Mother's virgin Son!
Who is, alone of womankind,
  Mother and virgin both in one!

Encircled by thy virgin band,
  Amid the lilies Thou art found,
For thy pure brides, with lavish hand,
  Scattering immortal graces round.

And still wherever Thou dost bend
  Thy lovely steps, O glorious King!
Virgins upon thy path attend,
  And hymns to thy high glory sing.

Keep us, O Purity divine!
 From every least corruption free;
Our every sense from sin refine,
 And purify our souls for Thee.

HYMN FOR HOLY WOMEN.

High let us all our voices raise
In that heroic woman's praise,
Whose name, with saintly glory bright
Shines in the starry realms of light.

Fill'd with a pure celestial glow,
She spurn'd all love of things below;
And heedless here on earth to stay,
Climb'd to the skies her toilsome way.

With fasts her body she subdued;
But fill'd her soul with prayer's sweet food,
In other worlds she tastes the bliss
For which she left the joys of this.

O Christ! the strength of all the strong,
To whom all our best deeds belong!
Through her prevailing prayers on high,
In mercy hear thy people's cry.

JERUSALEM, THOU CITY BLEST.

Jerusalem, thou city blest!
Dear vision of celestial rest!
Which, far above the starry sky,
Piled up with living stones on high,
Art, as a bride, encircled bright
With million angel forms of light.

Oh! wedded in a prosperous hour,
The Father's glory was thy dower;
The Spirit all His graces shed,
Thou peerless queen, upon thy head,
When Christ espoused thee for His bride,
O city bright and glorified!

Thy gates a pearly lustre pour;
Thy gates are open evermore;
And thither evermore draw nigh
All who for Christ have dared to die;
Or, smit with love of their dear Lord,
Have pains endured and joys abhorred.

Thou, too, O Church! which here we see,
No easy task hath builded thee.
Long did the chisels ring around!
Long did the mallet's blows rebound!
Long worked the head, and toiled the hand!
Ere stood thy stones as now they stand.

JERUSALEM.

Jerusalem, my happy home,
   How do I sigh for thee!
When shall my exile have an end?
   Thy joys when shall I see?

No sun, no moon in borrow'd light,
   Revolve thine hours away;
The Lamb on Calvary's mountain slain
   Is thy eternal day.

From every eye He wipes the tear,
   All sighs and sorrows cease;
No more alternate hope or fear,
   But everlasting peace.

When shall these eyes Thy heaven-built walls
   And pearly gates behold?
Thy bulwarks, with salvation strong,
   And streets of shining gold?

O Christ! do Thou my soul prepare
   For that bright home of love,
That I may see Thee and adore
   With all Thy saints above.

HYMN ON THE PASSION.

Go to dark Gethsemane,
  Ye that feel the tempter's power;
Your Redeemer's conflict see,
  Watch with Him one bitter hour:
Turn not from his griefs away,
Learn of Jesus Christ to pray.

Follow to the judgment-hall,
  View the Lord of life arraigned;
O the wormwood and the gall!
  O the pangs His soul sustained!
Shun not suffering, shame, or loss;
Learn of Him to bear the cross.

Calvary's mournful mountain climb;
  There, adoring at His feet,
Mark that miracle of time,
  God's own sacrifice complete.
"It is finished," hear Him cry,
Learn of Jesus Christ to die.

www.ingramcontent.com/pod-product-compliance
Lightning Source LLC
Chambersburg PA
CBHW031746230426
43669CB00007B/499